H

musings on the poems and places That made me a writer. With

SAID-SONGS

Thanks for all your good work and friendships

Essays on Poetry and Place

Jesse

August 23, 2022

MERCER UNIVERSITY PRESS

Endowed by

TOM WATSON BROWN
and
THE WATSON-BROWN FOUNDATION, INC.

SAID-SONGS

Essays on Poetry and Place

Jesse Graves

MERCER UNIVERSITY PRESS

Macon, Georgia

2021

MUP/ P628

© 2021 by Mercer University Press
Published by Mercer University Press
1501 Mercer University Drive
Macon, Georgia 31207

25 24 23 22 21   5 4 3 2 1

Books published by Mercer University Press are printed on acid-free paper
that meets the requirements of the American National Standard for
Information Sciences—Permanence of Paper for Printed Library Materials.

Printed and bound in the United States.

This book is set in the United States.

Cover/jacket design by Burt&Burt.

ISBN   978-0-88146-798-7
Cataloging-in-Publication Data is available from the Library of Congress

For Randall Wilhelm

Painter, Scholar,

Friend in any Noble Pursuit

Contents

Preface

The essays, interviews, and reviews collected here represent my experience as a young poet attempting to learn the mysteries and designs of poetry and to implement that learning into my own work. I received excellent formal training in reading and writing poems as an undergraduate and later a doctoral student at The University of Tennessee and as a Master of Fine Arts student at Cornell University. Yet I cannot help but feel that my travels through the vast territories of language have been idiosyncratic, quixotic even. One of the beauties and pleasures of reading literature, and poetry in particular, manifests in the unexpected turns one takes; one moment you are reading this book, and the next you have picked up a reference or an association that leads you to a different book. One soon recognizes that reading is a peregrine activity, and, as Robert Frost says, "way leads on to way." Though in reading, there is always circling back, and you will not be the same reader you were the first time you passed this fork in the road.

No two writers have read all the same books in the exact same order or felt the impact of the works in equal measure. We each have our own lineage of the imagination, and the art and nature we encounter helps to shape the signature our individual hands create. Imagination must move through a poem like blood through a body, the animating force unseen from the outside. Any part imagination fails to reach withers, and the whole poem suffers with it. If imagination is blood, inspiration is breath to a poem, equally essential, also unseen, also elusive of definition. No poet since William Butler Yeats has made a fuller study of the imagination than Kathleen Raine. She considers it a lost form of knowledge that once played a more central role in human understanding. The mystery of our lives has been increasingly, if unsatisfyingly, explained away through scientific and technological approaches. Raine believed that learning was essential to nurturing imagination, indicating that poems are made from other poems and that poets must take part in a tradition of perennial evaluation of what came before us so that we may render our own work.

Seamus Heaney called his first book of selected prose *Preoccupations*, and that seems to me the most useful way to think about my own essays. The essays collected in this volume bring together some of my most persistent interests, fascinations, and, well, preoccupations. These represent the writers, or the connections between writers, that I could not stop thinking about and felt compelled to try to understand through the steady concentration of analysis.

Perhaps prose is a poet's vernacular, the everyday speech with which we try to look at mystery with clarity, at ambiguity with order. The phrase "said-songs" comes from a title by the great poet A. R. Ammons, who was an essential early figure for me when I was a graduate student at Cornell University, where he was a professor for nearly forty years. Ammons writes about the music of speech as a pair of poems, "First Carolina Said-Song" and "Second Carolina Said-Song," from his 1966 collection *Northfield Poems*. In both poems, Ammons turns the voice over to characters, identified in parentheses beneath the titles, who speak in dialect. Reading those poems made a powerful impression on me about the music of language and of country speech. I used his phrase as a template when I wrote my own essay about dialect in poetry, which I called "Tennessee Said-Song: Dialect in Appalachian Poetry," and considered my own reluctance, and tentative attempts, to use the spoken vernacular in my poetry. I take Ammons's phrase as the title of this collection of prose explorations about the poetry and the places that have mattered most to me, all of which have given me the opportunity to work my humble shift in the service that Kathleen Raine calls "defending ancient springs."

Acknowledgments

I offer sincere thanks to the following editors, who encouraged the writing and publishing of many of the prose works in this book: Sandra Ballard, Maria Browning, Wayne Chapman, Nicole Drewitz-Crockett, John Lang, Michael Lofaro, Keith Moser, Charlotte Pence, Nathaniel Perry, Margaret Renkl, Sylvia Bailey Shurbutt, Zackery Vernon, Randall Wilhelm, and Marianne Worthington. Many other colleagues, friends, and professors played crucial roles in the composition and revision of these essays, and I owe special thanks to Bethann Bowman, Allen Dunn, Roger Gilbert, Thomas Alan Holmes, Marilyn Kallet, Charles Maland, Robert Morgan, the late and beloved Arthur Smith, and William Wright. I am grateful to the Literature & Language Department at East Tennessee State University for giving me a cast of colleagues I love and such a wonderful work-home, and for the opportunity to collaborate with so many talented graduate students through the years, including Brooke Bias, Jessica Hall, and Caleb McGhee, who all devoted many Research Assistant hours to this project. My wife Lisa and our daughter Chloe have offered encouragement and fun to every day of life, even the days spent working on essays.

Some works in this collection have been previously printed, sometimes in different forms, in the following publications:

"Awake in Their Wide Pastures: Formal Design in the Poems of Robert Morgan and Ron Rash." *Summoning the Dead: Critical Essays on Ron Rash*. Columbia: University of South Carolina Press, 2018.

"Tennessee Said-Song: Dialect in Appalachian Poetry." *Anthology of Appalachian Writers*, volume 2. Shepherdstown, WV: Shepherd University Press, 2009.

"Waltzing through the *Mysterium*: The Evolving Role of Music in the Poetry of David Bottoms." *South Carolina Review* 49, no. 1 (Fall 2016).

"The Wide Embrace of Jeff Daniel Marion." *Chapter 16*. 2013.

"Parallel Poetics: Ways of Seeing in James Agee and Federico García Lorca." *Let Us Now Praise Famous Men at 75: Anniversary Essays*, edited by Michael A. Lofaro. Knoxville: University of Tennessee Press, 2017.

"The Return of the Native Speaker: Maurice Manning's Dramatic Voices." *Iron Mountain Review* 29 (Summer 2013).

"The Single Seam in *The Double Dream of Spring:* Natural Sublime in the Poetry of John Ashbery." *South Carolina Review* 44, no. 1 (Fall 2011).

"On the Margins of the Writing World: K. S. M. McElmurray." *Iron Mountain Review* 31 (Fall 2018).

"Still Holding at the Seams: Magnolia Electric Co.'s *Josephine* and the Contemporary Poetic Sequence." In *The Poetics of American Song Lyrics*, edited by Charlotte Pence. Oxford: University of Mississippi Press, 2011.

"A Blind Work of Nature: The Ethics of Representing Beauty in *Let Us Now Praise Famous Men*." In *James Agee at 100: Centennial Essays*, edited by Michael A. Lofaro. Knoxville: University of Tennessee Press, 2012.

"James Agee's 'Knoxville: Summer, 1915." *Still: The Journal* (Fall 2017).

Letters to the Dead: A Memoir by Jeff Daniel Marion. Review. *Appalachian Journal*. 2015.

Lambs of Men: A Novel by Charles Dodd White. Review. *Journal of Appalachian Studies*. 2012.

Long Man: A Novel by Amy Greene. Review. *Appalachian Heritage*. 2014.

Mother Land: Poems by Linda Parsons Marion. Review. *Louisiana Literature*. 2010.

Oblivion Banjo: The Poetry of Charles Wright by Charles Wright. Review. *Chapter 16*. 2020.

Preface to *Grass Chapels: New & Selected Poems* by William Wright. Macon, GA: Mercer University Press, 2021.

Charles Wright: A Companion to the Late Poetry, 1988–2007 by Robert D. Denham. Review. *Appalachian Journal*. 2009.

Still in Print: The Southern Novel Today, edited by Jan Nordby Gretlund. Review. *Appalachian Journal*. 2012.

In Exchange: Interviews with William Wright for *Town Creek Poetry*; with Denton Loving for *Chapter 16*; with Nathaniel Perry for *Hampden-Sydney Poetry Review*; with Alexandra Taylor for *Roanoke Review*; with Linda Parsons for *Chapter 16*.

PART I

1

The Lyric: A Personal History

I. To Crawl in Among the Machinery

In his 1965 essay, "Structure and Style in the Greater Romantic Lyric,"
M. H. Abrams surmises the difference between the "local poem"—a
phrase he borrows from Samuel Johnson—of the seventeenth and early
eighteenth centuries and a new kind of poem that began in the 1790s and
embodies some of the greatest achievements of Coleridge, Wordsworth,
Keats, and Shelley. Abrams calls this new type of poem "the greater Romantic lyric" and notes that chief among its qualities is a pattern, an "out-
in-out process in which the mind confronts nature and the interplay constitutes the poem."[1] Prior to the invention of this new mode of lyric, the
"local poem" was merely a descriptive passage in which the speaker would
look upon a natural setting, attempt to accurately describe it, and then relate it to some personal memory or moral sentiment. The interplay between mind and environment is what makes the greater Romantic lyric
distinct from earlier forms of lyric poetry. Abrams suggests that the new
approach found its origins in Coleridge's disdain for dualisms of any
kind—for instance, between body and mind, thought and action, or interior and exterior. The greater Romantic lyric initiated an expressive mode

---

[1] M. H. Abrams, "Style and Structure in the Greater Romantic Lyric," in
The Correspondent Breeze (New York: Norton, 1984), 78.

of poetry that integrates the speaker of a poem with his or her environment, thus enabling the poem to become what Wallace Stevens, the great twentieth century Romantic, called "the act of the mind" in his poem "Of Modern Poetry."

The poems in my first poetry collection, *Tennessee Landscape with Blighted Pine*, aspire to the same integrated relationship between description and perception, in which the eye of the speaker observes, the mind responds and interacts, and then the eye sees again, this time with an enhanced perspective. My poems often have definite physical settings, and I try very hard to create the environments in which the occasions of the poems take place, but I am also invested in the interplay between the descriptive setting and the experience of the speaker. Setting in my poems is rarely simply backdrop; it often provides stimulus to the mind or actions of the speaker. In his book *The Idea of Lyric*, W. R. Johnson discusses the way in which lyric imagery reaches beyond the doctrine of mimesis into the complex exchange of artistic creation:

> When Paul Cezanne designed that garment tossed randomly on that chair, he was not trying to reproduce, to represent, the naturalistic look of that garment on that chair; rather, he was, like the cave dweller and the Greek sculptor, patterning what he and, potentially, all humans see and feel and think about their lives; he was, in the simplest and profoundest sense of the word, *helping* us to *see* chairs and garments as they are, life as it is, ourselves as we are.[2]

Poetry is a reimagining as well as a reflection of an occasion, and a strong poem must be able to describe its environment accurately and provide therein the canvas for the lived experience of its speaker.

The lyric poem in the early twenty-first century resembles the native poplar tree, which thrives because of its many branchings. In fact, a great deal of the lyric mode's strength derives from the varieties of interpretation and implementation forced upon it by poets with considerably differing sensibilities. A definite ambition for my work is that it demonstrates range within certain parameters, that it engages the means of lyric poetry as well as the historical accumulation of years of engaged and attentive reading. A lyric poet's voice emerges out of a tradition of reading and responding to consequential poems that precede him or her, and in my case, this goes as

---

[2] W. R. Johnson, *The Idea of Lyric* (Berkeley: University of California Press, 1982), 13.

far back as the ancient Greek lyrics of Sappho and Archilochus and continues through an ongoing engagement with the current issues of such literary journals as *Hudson Review*, *Prairie Schooner*, and *Southern Poetry Review*.

How does a first book come together? How can a poet acquire the tools needed for this ancient trade? How should a poet integrate the variety of the world—the physical, emotional, spiritual, historical world—into his or her work? In action and in reflection, I have tried to understand these and other questions. I have narrowed my field of readings and experiences to represent those that most serve as influence and inspiration for my own writing. I intend to place my poems within a framework and a lineage of the poetry I have admired and from which I have learned my art and my craft.

A primary drive in my poems has been a pursuit of the question of what to do with the memories of people and places that are now lost to me. This is the essence of elegiac poetry but also one of the historical foundations of the lyric mode. I have paid special attention to those modern and contemporary poets who are most open to regarding loss and to identifying the emotions brought to bear on the self when loss is confronted. Two central concerns in my poetry are the grief at losing a loved family member and the sense of upheaval when a landscape or an entire community gets displaced, which happened to my immediate ancestors when the Tennessee Valley Authority flooded miles and miles of farmland for the construction of a series of dams in the 1930s. Poets who examine loss on a personal level, as well as on the level of community and landscape, emerge as the greatest influence on my work, and I have studied some of them, such as Charles Wright and Tomas Tranströmer, in great detail. I have tried to learn from these master poets how to avoid the pitfall of sentimentality, how to approach material that involves significant emotional risk without falling into an exaggerated sense of import.

In his essay, "The Pastoral: First and Last Things," David Baker considers the contemporary misuse of the term "pastoral" as a noun, such that it is a catchall for any poem with nature in it. Baker gives a long historical account of the form, with a useful view of how and where it began:

> Theocritus and his pastoral lyrics are a slightly more recent development than the three ur-forms of the lyric. We might date the erotic poem back to Sappho, on Lesbos, around 600 BC. We can take the written elegy back at least to Simonides of Keos, in the

early 500s BC, although we can trace the choral elegy back to Archilochus in the latter half of the eighth century BC, on Paros. And Pindar formed his great odes in the late 400s BC. Theocritus was born in about 300 BC.[3]

For Baker, the continuing value of the pastoral is its adaptability to any age, but I find the persistence and continuity of the genre, especially in modified forms, to be its most striking characteristic. The pastoral impulse was originally one of local celebration and was then turned inward toward a more meditative form by the same need that created the greater Romantic lyric. The permanence of the lyric mode of poetry derives from its propensity for looking back and for granting perspective on time and loss from the present.

In the preface to her 1995 book *Sappho Is Burning*, Page duBois makes a remarkable claim on the importance of historical understanding. She says of Sappho:

> She stands for me a sign of why we still need history, why we should not be satisfied with a one-dimensional, atemporal, global postmodern culture, why the study of history, of distant times and distant places can provide us the experience of difference, a productive memory of latent fragments of human being, now remote but recoverable through our inquiry into what we have lost.[4]

Sappho remains a major voice in the evolution of lyric poetry not simply because she appears so near the beginning of the lineage but because she presents a recognizable perspective, in spite of her work arriving to us in fragments. Sappho predates the pastoral of Theocritus, but she introduces the poem of personal will and desire, the poem of an individual voice. The great lyric impulses toward reflection, meditation, remembrance, celebration, and heightened sensitivity all emerge in Sappho and become a thread in the master narrative of history, of which literary history and the evolution of language and thought are a part.

The Irish poet and Nobel Prize-winner Seamus Heaney, in a sequence of elegies for his mother, titled "Clearances," and for his father,

---

[3] David Baker, "The Pastoral: First and Last Things," in *Radiant Lyre: Essays on Lyric Poetry*, ed. David Baker and Ann Townsend (St. Paul: Graywolf, 2007), 135.

[4] Page duBois, *Sappho Is Burning* (Chicago: University of Chicago Press, 1995), ix.

titled "The Stone Verdict," examines the vacancy left in the absence of his parents and considers the many ambiguities of elderly parent/grown child relationships. Heaney never settles for easy resolutions and rejects doctrinal comforts; critic Jahan Ramazani, in his chapter on Seamus Heaney in *The Poetry of Mourning*, states that Heaney "refuses to redeem death in beautiful poetry,"[5] and he finds the force of Heaney's elegies in that refusal. American poets Jack Gilbert and Mark Doty have written powerful and affecting elegies for a spouse and a life partner, respectively, and A. R. Ammons and Marie Howe have written about the loss of siblings and other family relations. In his poem "By Small and Small: Midnight to Four A.M.," Jack Gilbert writes of the final hours of his wife Michiko's life and recognizes a painful instance in reflection, an opportunity for embrace that he could not see in the moment of grief. I quote the brief poem in its entirety from *Refusing Heaven*:

> For eleven years I have regretted it,
> regretted that I did not do what
> I wanted to do as I sat there those
> four hours watching her die. I wanted
> to crawl in among the machinery
> and hold her in my arms, knowing
> the elementary, leftover bit of her
> mind would dimly recognize it was me
> carrying her to where she was going.[6]

The speaker in Gilbert's poem connects the full weight of his grief to an opportunity he missed, and it is one of the key functions of the elegy to locate an abstract sense of loss with a particular moment or image, tracing as far back as Shelley's evocations of the young Keats in *Adonais*. Perhaps Gilbert's poem most resembles Thomas Hardy's elegies for his late wife in *Poems of 1912-13*, such as "At Castle Boterel" and "Her Last Drive."

Robert Morgan, once called "the Poet Laureate of Appalachia," writes in his poem "Wild Peavines" of the changing landscapes of the

---

[5] Jahan Ramazani, *Poetry of Mourning: The Modern Elegy from Hardy to Heaney* (Chicago: University of Chicago Press, 1994), 346.

[6] Jack Gilbert, *Refusing Heaven* (New York: Knopf, 2005), 14.

Mountain South and how they result in absences_that represent a lost history. Morgan's poem opens with the image of how the Appalachian Mountains must have appeared to the first inhabitants, covered thick with wild peavines and their heavy scent. The speaker struggles to create a picture of this scene, and finally says,

> But hardest of all to see
> is how such profusion...
> could vanish,
> so completely disappear that
> you must look through several valleys
> to find a sprig or strand of wild peavine
> curling on a weedstalk.[7]

Once again, Abrams's "Style and Structure in the Greater Romantic Lyric" offers a useful analysis for the connections made in the mind of the speaker. Abrams claims that "among Romantic poets, the distinction between self and not-self tends to disappear when confronted with natural landscapes."[8] Abrams's claim resonates with the conclusion of Morgan's poem, in which the speaker imagines the near-extinct peavines as representations of his family ancestors, "like some word from a lost language / once flourishing on every tongue."[9]

A primary concern in the poetry that has most influenced my work is the use of landscape and sense of place in lyric poetry, specifically the ways in which poets identify strongly with a particular landscape or locale. Literary examples date back to the Greeks, but it is with William Wordsworth and his era of Romantic poets that I begin to trace the line of influence and continuity that carries through very contemporary work such as Robert Morgan's and Charles Wright's. My second area of concern is deeply intertwined with the first and deals with the elegy as a mode of lyric writing. Again, the literary tradition of the elegy is essentially as old as literature itself, and I view it as one of the foundational impulses of making art in any form or medium. One of the earliest types of elegy is the "pas-

---

[7] Robert Morgan, "Wild Peavines," in *The Strange Attractor: New and Selected Poems* (Baton Rouge: Louisiana State University Press, 2005).

[8] Abrams, "Style and Structure," 98.

[9] Morgan, "Wild Peavines," 126.

toral elegy," elucidated by Peter Sacks in his indispensable book *The English Elegy*, and many versions of the genre elegize natural objects and animals as well as human lives. Ecological poets such as Gary Snyder and Robert Bly represent this aspect of the landscape elegy. They are contemporary examples of poets whose ideas about Nature interconnect so deeply with their ideas about human life that the two are virtually inseparable; in their work, what is lost in Nature is also lost to humanity.

The mode of the elegy has a long history that far predates English poetry, with roots in Homer, Greek lyric poets and dramatists such as Sappho and Aeschylus, and the eclogues of Theocritus and Virgil. The meanings and associations for the term itself have changed many times throughout the years. In Greek, the term *elegy*, or *elegeia*, referred to a type of meter rather than to a convention of content, such as the lament or mourning poem, as the term has come to represent in the English tradition. However, the manner of content—the conscious (and conscientious) mourning over a loss of life, a misplaced belief, an irretrievable time or experience—existed in both Greek and Roman literatures, particularly in the form of epitaphs, as it has in representative literature of all times and societies. In Old English poetry, one finds elements of the elegiac lament in *The Wanderer* and *The Seafarer* as well as in the touching scene of burial and mourning, with its justification and consolation, near the end of *Beowulf* after the hero has died. Less pronounced examples exist in Middle English poetry, in the *Pearl* text and in lyrics such as "The Grave," though not notably in Chaucer's *Canterbury Tales*. The elegy then made a powerful reemergence and a permanent return in the sixteenth century with the work of Edmund Spenser and Sir Philip Sidney, poets who revisited and modified the classical elegiac form. The elegiac impulse is tightly woven into the framework of lyric poetry, but one also finds it in the plays of William Shakespeare, as when Hamlet mourns the death of his father, and as the emotional centerpiece of novels from Emily Bronte's *Wuthering Heights* (1847) to W. G. Sebald's *Austerlitz* (2001), with such definitive examples as Virginia Woolf's *To the Lighthouse* (1927) and Ernest Hemingway's *A Farewell to Arms* (1929) between them.

The key elements of elegiac art exist in perfect communion with certain core primal elements of human experience, yet there is no simplicity in the highest forms of elegy, because the experience must make the complicated transferal into art. This constitutes "the work of mourning" Sigmund Freud refers to in the essay "Mourning and Melancholia," and it is the formalization of human feelings that makes the elegy such a centripetal force in English language poetry. The elegist confronts a seemingly impossible, certainly inevitable task: the event of loss must be articulated and made comprehensible to the audience, regardless of its magnitude or proximity. Every sufferer of loss must absorb or deny the event, must attempt—or not—to work through it, and the elegist must carry this organic process through an artificial gateway into the realm of the poem itself, the poem in response to the loss. The difficulty facing the poet includes finding the proper register, the adequate image, and the correct measure of emotion, a process Heaney, the greatest of contemporary elegists, addresses in his essay "The Interesting Case of Nero, Chekhov's Cognac, and the Knocker." Heaney recounts an evening in 1972 in which he and friends have planned to make music together, but as they are set to begin a bomb blasts through Belfast, and he writes about the forced considerations he must give to the "embarrassment of the poet because of the artfulness of his art"[10] in the wake of such destruction. The German theorist Theodor Adorno wrestled with this issue in his 1949 essay "After Auschwitz," famously stating that he now believes it is "barbaric" to try to "make sense out of the victims' suffering."[11] This comment resonates deeply after a century of such prodigious destruction of human life and such easily attained, readily commercialized comfort and diversion. The contemporary poet must engage this problem—as Heaney does by claiming that within lyric poetry one finds "a sensation of liberation and abundance which is the antithesis of every hampered and deprived condition"[12]—and must take care not to fall into hollow conventions.

II. Poems and Places:
Central Images and Locales

In his now-classic 1986 volume *Unattainable Earth*, Polish Nobel Laureate Czeslaw Milosz includes a prose meditation on what the poem of the future will contain:

> What will the future of poetry be, which I think of but will never

---

[10] Seamus Heaney, "The Interesting Case of Nero, Chekhov's Cognac, and the Knocker," in *The Government of the Tongue* (New York: FSG, 1995), xviii.

[11] Theodore Adorno, "After Auschwitz," in *Negative Dialectics*, trans. E. B. Ashton (New York: Continuum, 1973), 361.

[12] Heaney, "The Interesting Case of Nero," xviii.

know? I know it is attainable because I experienced brief moments when it almost created itself under my pen, only to disappear immediately. The rhythm of the body will be in it, heartbeat, pulse, sweating, menstrual flow, the gluiness of sperm, the squatting position at urinating, the movements of the intestines, together with the sublime needs of the spirit, and our duality will find its form in it, without renouncing one zone or the other.[13]

Poems are placed objects. A poet must locate his or her poems. They exist in both the eye and the ear of the reader, yet they also must originate from a source within the poet, and I have tried to bear Milosz's credo in mind: that the authentic poem must attend to the body and spirit; the past, the present, and the future; the erotic as well as the contemplative; the ode along with the elegy. The model Milosz proposes belongs not only to the future; it has existed at least since Wordsworth's sublime revelation at the Simplon Pass in *The Prelude* and Keats's articulation of "Negative Capability" in a letter to his brothers, and it continues down through Robert Bly's conception of "two-fold consciousness." The greatest poets of the lyric tradition have recognized and embraced the power of mystery and contradiction, and I have aimed to keep my poems, while ultimately representative and rooted in image, experience, and narrative memory, open to the same power of the unknown.

My first poetry collection, *Tennessee Landscape with Blighted Pine*, includes the title poem, a longer meditative poem that breaks into shorter thematic sections. Many of the recurrent themes in the manuscript appear within this single poem, and the poem covers a great deal of narrative time and geographic space. The poem opens in present tense, with the speaker as a young man standing in a field on his family farm remembering time spent there when he was a boy. It then moves in sections back through the intervening years and the constancy of that field in his life, passing through his imagining of how the region must have appeared to his ancestors who settled in the area more than two hundred years before. The poem examines the physical terrain but also the speaker's personal longings for, and doubts about, a continuity with the land, while looking at contradictions in his own being and grasping for the ghosts of his lineage that he feels as a tangible presence around him. These same concerns are voiced again in my poems "Digging the Pond" and "Firing Order."

---

[13] Czeslaw Milosz, *Unattainable Earth* (New York: Ecco Press, 1986), 33.

Landscape and particularity of setting is a key to the tradition of Appalachian poetry, but another primary model for this strain of my poetry is the Spanish poet Antonio Machado. Machado imbues an austerity of vision in the landscapes of his native Castile, which not only creates richly textured geographic canvases but also lends a spiritual clarity to his insights. In his 1906 poem "Portrait," Machado reflects back to his childhood and how those events shaped him as a poet and prepared him for a life of close attention:

I scorn the ballads of loud tenors as hollow
as a choir of crickets singing to the moon.
I stop to note the voices from their echo
and among those voices listen to only one.[14]

Machado reminds us that poetry is not only a search for beauty but also a search for truth, and that spectacle and volume often obscure the kind of truth that close attention can reveal.

Contemporary European poetry also has provided many important models for my poems and for my thinking about poetry. Tomas Tranströmer's long poem from 1974, titled *Baltics*, has been an enabling piece of writing for me, both in its evocation of family history and personal narrative and as an approach toward understanding oneself as a thread in an unrecoverable lineage. The poem opens not with a speaker but with an image that is as much temporal as it is spatial:

It was before the age of the radio masts.

Grandfather was a new-made pilot. In the almanac he wrote down the
    vessels he piloted—
names, destinations, drafts.
Examples from 1884:
Steam Tiger   Capt. Rowan   16 ft   Hull Gefle Furusund

Brigg Ocean   Capt. Anderson   8 ft   Sandofjord Hernosand
    Furusund

---

[14] Antonio Machado, *Border of a Dream* (Port Townsend: Copper Canyon, 2004), 139.

Steamer St Petersburg   Capt. Libenburg   11 ft   Stettin Libau
Sandhamn[15]

These first seven lines evoke an entire world: a historical moment, an individual in that time, his vocation, and the grain of the language he wrote and spoke, as well as an expressive poetic voice and rhythm for the poem. The speaker does not appear until near the end of the second of the poem's six sections, in an extended version of the "out-in-out process" of the greater Romantic lyric. The poem moves along an associative, imagistic path toward a deep understanding of the speaker's relationship with what came before him. My poem "Tennessee Landscape with Blighted Pine" was definitely influenced by reading *Baltics* and by the techniques Tranströmer uses to develop the consciousness of a speaker by first introducing the natural setting and family lineage that gave shape to the consciousness.

My evocation of landscape is part of an attempt to access "something more than nature in the grove," as Coleridge says in *Christabel*. Nature is both patterned and ever-changing and provides a perfect model for the workings of poetry; A. R. Ammons has claimed that every poem is like a walk, and no two walks are ever alike, even on the same path at the same time every day. Charles Wright has called landscape interaction the "lever of transcendence," suggesting that it provides the only imagery we have with which to imagine the world beyond our lives. Landscape and elegy have a deep resonance with one another in the history of the lyric poem, as though the content of elegy needed the imagery of pastoral, and the timelessness of pastoral needed the tone of elegy. I wouldn't necessarily call my poems pastorals, as the pastoral suggests permanence, an unchanging quality, in nature that my experience contradicts. The pastoral does, however, examine the relationship between people and place (both "landscape," which is cultivated, and "nature," which is uncultivated), and that is a key component to my poetry.

I feel specifically connected to the place where I grew up, a small farming community in northeastern Tennessee, about forty miles north of Knoxville, and I'm sure that bond comes through in my work. My experience in this regard is becoming increasingly rare in America, in that I grew up in a community that my ancestors helped to establish in the 1780s.

---

[15] Tomas Tranströmer, *Baltics* (Stockholm: Bonnier, 1974), 7.

Johannes Sebastian Graff came to America from the German Palatinate in 1730 and lived in Pennsylvania and then western North Carolina. His brother, Jacob Graff, Jr., built the house in Philadelphia and rented the rooms to Thomas Jefferson where he wrote the Declaration of Independence. Johannes's daughter married another German immigrant named Henry Scharp and moved in 1784 to what was then a western outpost, which they named Scharps Fort. Old Johannes and a couple of his sons followed them in a few years to that settlement at the convergence of the Clinch and Powell rivers, and the younger men took on English-sounding names, Sharp and Graves. Johannes died in Sharps Chapel, Tennessee, in 1804 at the age of 102, refusing to ever change his name. My family was moved from that particular piece of land—nearly a thousand acres of river bottom for farming and timber—in the mid-1930s when the TVA built Norris Dam, so I did not grow up on the same ground they cleared but only a few miles from it. Much of this history forms the context for my poem, "Tennessee Landscape with Blighted Pine," which attempts to understand some of the mystery of feeling that one belongs to a place.

I live in East Tennessee again, now in Johnson City, though previously I lived for four years in Ithaca, New York, and for one year in New Orleans. I was inspired by both of those places. Ithaca is fairly Edenic with its Farmer's Market, its intellectual diversity, and its abundance of used book stores and green spaces; New Orleans felt mythic and alive to me in ways that I am trying still to figure out, and yet I never exactly felt at home in either of them. Both of those cities have been settings for a number of my recent poems and will probably continue to be—it's not uncommon for an image or an event to wait several years before presenting itself as a poem to me. However, my understanding of the history and development of Ithaca and New Orleans is so much less ingrained than my sense of the scope of life in East Tennessee, and I think that whatever is most deeply ingrained within a poet is his or her truest subject matter.

My poems rely more heavily on setting, on the physical space in which the poem's action takes place, than most contemporary poetry. Landscape dominates the imagery of my work because I have spent so much time in the midst of it—there are no visible neighbors from the house where I grew up. Had I been raised in Memphis, Tennessee, instead of Sharps Chapel, Tennessee, I don't doubt that the settings of my poems would be different, but I suspect that physical surroundings would remain just as important to the imagery. I obsess over place and location in poetry, the grain of specificity and shared history, which draws me naturally to Appalachian writers like Jeff Daniel Marion, Robert Morgan, and Ron Rash but also gives me access to a poet like Charles Olson, with his own obsession with Gloucester, Massachusetts, that I might not otherwise have. I do recognize the risk of cliché, the risk of pat responses in using landscape imagery so heavily, but I think there is also a deeper level of resonance in a solitary speaker in a field that reverberates back through Theocritus—the impact of the environment on a poet in its midst is present in every culture that has ever produced poetry.

Landscape interactions in poetry provide a means to translate belief, doubt, and relational consciousness—the probing aspects of a speaker's personality—into tangible imagery. My poem "Nightjar Songs," like much of the writing in *Tennessee Landscape*, considers the vastness of the unknowable, particularly in light of how little we can apprehend with certainty even of the close at hand. The poem gains access to its subject matter through physical description, searching unsuccessfully for what Frances Ferguson calls "the composable scene."[16] The speaker of the poem reflects his own internal disorder against the comparative order of the external and can almost, though not quite, accept that both are part of some larger "design." The poem takes part in the changing nature of the sublime, namely that in the contemporary world the monumental may be felt in even so contained a landscape as a front yard. I hope that both the word and concept of "design" echo the contemporary debate surrounding the "intelligent design" of the universe by some force greater than cosmic accident, about which the speaker remains skeptical, as well as the literary precedent of Robert Frost's classic poem "Design" and its ambivalent view on divine intervention and governance.

Much contemporary American poetry, in a gesture of response to an increasingly technological way of life, sacrifices depth of attention and locality of focus for an aesthetics of rapid dislocation and emotional detachment. Younger American poets like Matthea Harvey and Joshua Clover write poems that respond with frenetic juxtapositions of scene and image and that constantly undercut any gesture toward emotional investment or attachment. In a prominent essay titled "Fear of Narrative and the Skittery

---

[16] For a closer look at Frances Ferguson's work on the sublime, see my essay on John Ashbery's poetry later in this volume.

Poem of Our Moment," published in the March 2006 issue of *Poetry* magazine, Tony Hoagland diagnoses the situation:

Generally speaking, this time could be characterized as one of great invention and playfulness. Simultaneously, it is also a moment of great aesthetic self-consciousness and emotional removal. Systematic development is out; obliquity, fracture, and discontinuity are in. Especially among young poets, there is a widespread mistrust of narrative forms and, in fact, a pervasive sense of the inadequacy or exhaustion of all modes other than the associative. Under the label of "narrative," all kinds of poetry currently get lumped misleadingly together: not just story but discursion, argument, even descriptive lyrics. They might better be called the "Poetries of Continuity."

Many contemporary poems move from image to image with video game-like intensity without presenting any point of authority or consequence, often with no discernible speaker. Whereas Hoagland finds the essential "skittery"-ness of contemporary poetry located in its dissociative tendencies, I find the problem of emotional removal exists in direct correspondence to the author's glibness about the subject matter of the poem. Hoagland rightly indicates that Matthea Harvey has written "a poem, we are never allowed to forget, about pronouns." In other words, nothing is at stake in the poem, except the chance that the humor may fall flat. Harvey's poem doesn't risk anything emotionally, and, in fact, it doesn't even present a speaker. Such poetry is a continuation of the assault on the "Lyric I" initiated by Language poetry throughout the 1970s and '80s. I agree with Hoagland's conclusion that this approach to poetry, in an attempt to pay homage to life in an elliptical cultural moment, risks a commitment to being ultimately about nothing, an inadvertent homage to triviality.

In his book *Memory and Enthusiasm*, W. S. Di Piero, in a discussion of Keats and the Italian Nobel Laureate Eugenio Montale, writes, "A major lyric poet is one who not only explores in a sustained way, but who also tries to determine and *place*, the graduated registers of actual and metaphysical reality, and who is willing to assert the precise relations between the worlds of the living and of the dead, the relations between the here-and-now and the *aldila*."[17] Many of the current trends and fashions of contemporary poetry suggest potential for the birth of another age of satire.

---

[17] W. S. Di Piero, "Southern," in *Memory and Enthusiasm: Essays, 1975–1985* (Princeton: Princeton UP, 1989), 176.

After two decades of political absurdity and ineptitude, and a near constant threat of economic collapse, it is not hard to see how a turn toward satire could happen. The history of Latin and English poetry would seem to indicate such a move toward the satirical as a natural development following an age of great, sustained lyric output, though that dialectic must be resisted if American poetry is to avoid a similar dead end. I feel that contemporary poetry is strongest when it averts the postmodern impulse toward dislocation and detachment. The contrast between the "skittery poem of our moment" and the poems of our finest writers of the personal lyric, such as Jack Gilbert, Louise Glück, and B. H. Fairchild, who make the explorations into the actual and the metaphysical that Di Piero elucidates, only exemplifies the strength of a poetics of continuity and the permanence of lyric poetry.

III. Dynamic Alertness:
Forms and Measures

In his essay, "Improvisations on Form and Measure," poet Charles Wright states, "In poems, all considerations are considerations of form."[18] I believe that I have always recognized this deep in the back stretches of my mind, but I had never quite brought it to bear regarding my own poems, had never articulated it in practice before taking on the challenge of working in forms. My mature thinking on poetry was shaped early and irreversibly by William Wordsworth's claim in his "Preface Attached to *Lyrical Ballads*" to write with "language really used by men." This led me to conclude that the most natural voice, and the most natural forms, would be the only acceptable route for my poems and that the most natural form would be, of course, free verse. All the contemporary poets I admired, such as James Wright, Robert Bly, Lucille Clifton, and Mary Oliver, wrote in the language of everyday speech, and they had rejected the formal constraints of earlier generations. I am tempted to say that I accepted free verse as the water in which I would swim and never thought twice about it, but in looking back I do remember working at forms as an undergraduate, even winning the poetry prize for formal poems with a pantoum I had written outside of class. I suppose questions of form have been with me since the

---

[18] Charles Wright, "Improvisations on Form and Measure," in *Halflife* (Ann Arbor: University Michigan Press, 1988), 3.

17

beginning of my serious work at poetry, along with an interest in determining whether formal verse could accomplish anything that free verse could not. In attempt after attempt in my recent work, I found that in holding a poem to form, something happened each time that surprised me, as in the case of "Vista" with the line about Cezanne. Some of the surprises contributed more than others, and some poems responded better to being held in form. Ultimately, I feel that my range as a poet has broadened considerably during this concentrated examination of poetic forms.

Even when I do not use fixed measures or recurring patterns in my poems, I am very conscious of the music a phrase must make to enliven the language and give the poem a sense of architectural design. I pay close attention to syllable counts and line lengths in my free verse poems as much as in my formal poems. For instance, in my poem "Mother's Milk," the voice of the speaker changes in tonality, moving from a documentary-style cataloguing to conversational address to the fragmentary mode of internal dialogue, yet the six distinct sections of the poem maintain a shapeliness, a consistency of design, that balances the movements in the voice. I continue this attention to formal design in later poems, such as "Time's Weave" from my second collection, *Basin Ghosts*. "Time's Weave" is also a poem inspired by time spent with my mother, which I developed in a strict syllabic pattern, alternating ten-syllable and seven-syllable line counts. The use of a regular syllabic count creates a feeling of directed forward movement but without the sense of lock-step marching that a pattern of fixed stresses can force upon a poem.

Tennessee Landscape with Blighted Pine includes poems about my mother, my wife, and my daughter, three of the keys to my life and the meaning it has taken on over the years, as well as poems for my father and my uncle Gerald, whose work ethics and personal kindnesses were two of my earliest inspirations for poetry. A handful of poems address, directly and indirectly, my frustration with the state of recent American politics, particularly its encouragement of vacant consumerism. Certain poems pursue my ongoing fascination with a mode of poetry that M. H. Abrams has called "landscape autobiography" and the rooted-ness created by generations of one family settled in a single place. Several poems bring together experiences in which memory and bodies of water converge to form a counterbalance to my continued examination of the imagery of open fields and forests. The poems in my first book also represent an effort to employ a variety of available sources of materials as well as a broad range of stylistic and tonal possibilities, and several of the poems admit an undercurrent of humor or irony, an important part of my personal sensibility that did not develop in my writing for many years. Poems such as "Sparrow" and "Elegy for the Hay Rake" gesture toward a wry understanding that poetry should not collapse under its own weight. The variation in appearance could give a reader the sense of a poet struggling for a form, or for a personal style, but each of the poems in *Tennessee Landscape* has been carefully weighed and measured against the other poems in the collection with a definite attention to coherence and sustained statement. The content of each poem determined its own form—some calling for rigorous constraints and some calling for greater openness and flexibility—and I believe that my openness to form granted the poems the freedom they needed to emerge.

Certain individual poems bear the mark of the poets I was reading at the time I wrote them. "River Gods" was inspired by Yusef Komunyakaa's poem "Confluence" from his collection *Thieves of Paradise*, especially in its evocation of the mythos linking water and memory and its layering of time and experience through the image of a bridge. Komunyakaa's lines, "So deep in the lore, / there's only tomorrow where darkness / splinters & wounds the bird of paradise,"[19] resonated with my sense of how a space that had shaped my consciousness also had a history, some factual and some mythic, that shaped my history as well. My return to Knoxville, Tennessee, as a doctoral student has brought me back into contact with people and places that I knew intimately for the first twenty-five years of my life, and particularly the formative years of my young adulthood. In my poem "River Gods," and a number of others, I confront feelings that seem planted in the place, as natural and present as shadows, but that really belong to an earlier time and to an earlier version of myself. The form for "River Gods" emerged from my reading of Komunyakaa but also out of a sense of organic and intuitive shape for the content of the poem. I chose a tercet line rather than Komunyakaa's couplet because my poem lingers with certain images and scenes of action longer, and it relies more on the establishment of a narrative movement through time, though I do think both poems develop in a similar manner, particularly in the way their conclusions leave a sense of unresolved mystery behind human actions and desires.

---

[19] Yusef Komunyakaa, "Confluence," in *Thieves of Paradise* (Hanover: Wesleyan University Press, 1998), 14.

Robert Hass's poems in *Human Wishes* and *Sun Under Wood* were models for my poems "Mother's Milk" and "His Confession," both of which experiment with shape and movement and also with a tonal looseness that moves from the weighty to the wry and back again. I have also considered Hass's use of the prose poem, as well as his hybrid form of long-lined lyric poems that embody the attention to image and a kind of spatial rhythm yet retain some of the expansiveness of a prose line. In the sequence of poems that opens Hass's volume *Human Wishes,* including "Spring Drawing," "Spring Rain," "Late Spring," and "Spring Drawing 2," the hybrid line creates a texture distinct from verse lines and from prose, and it embodies the value placed on imagery and rhythm, which Hass emphasizes in his seminal collection of essays titled *Twentieth Century Pleasures.*

My poems "Storm Lines" and "Echolalia" show the importance of Brenda Hillman's idea of putting "air" into the lines of poems and giving a voice to the silence and white space inherent in every poem. Her collections *Cascadia* and *Loose Sugar* exemplify how a concern with natural elements and cycles suggests a model for poetics. "Storm Lines" particularly owes a debt to Hillman, as it gave me the opportunity to weight each line by its rhythm rather than using conventional punctuation, and to articulate gestures in less familiar or comfortable phrasings. Reading the manuscript as a whole, however, I believe that the poems cohere under a single voice, a single vision for how the world operates, and that the more experimental poems do not represent a break from my style or manner but rather are a promising sign of enlargement, forerunners of a more expansive poetic accomplishment.

As with many things, Walt Whitman has written as movingly as any poet about the embodiment of form in the 1855 version of *Song of Myself,* in Section 27, just after he has urged his unseen listener to embrace the "puzzle of puzzles, / And that we call Being":

[27]
To be in any form, what is that?...
If nothing lay more develop'd the quahuag and its callous
    shell were enough.

Mine is no callous shell,
I have instant conductors all over me whether I pass or

stop,
They seize every object and lead it harmlessly through me.

I merely stir, press, feel with my fingers, and am happy,
To touch my person to some one else's is about as much as
        I can stand.

This is Whitman's vision of form as it exists organically within the human body, exactly where Robert Pinsky believes the voice of poetry originates (Pinsky locates the initial stirrings of a poem in the thorax). The poet William Matthews once famously wrote, "I am in my poems because I am in my life." I have tried to write my poems from a coherent perspective, communicating my perceptions of the people, places, and ideas that I encounter through imaginative renderings and explorations. This is not the same thing as keeping a journal, in part because it is intended for an audience of readers and also because I have given the experiences form. It is not relevant whether the material is autobiographical or not, but only whether the evocations are truthful to human experience and understanding. I am increasingly convinced that a personal speaker, with an implied or addressed listener, is the essence of the lyric poem.

As a child, I was something of a collector, of baseball cards, Hot Wheels cars, little things like that, but also a collector of information: I would learn things like the habitat, hunting methods, and war decorations for every Native American tribe; I could identify cars from a certain period just by seeing the position of the headlights or the shape of a fender; I memorized batting averages and earned run averages for every Major League baseball team. I think this tendency in my mind plays out in a pronounced way in some of my strongest poetry—the collection and re-configuration of details, of "time and materials," to borrow a concept from Robert Hass. My poems "At Seven" and "Equations" both register these propensities. I feel that I am working now on a canvas that is both broader and somehow deeper in perspective than I have been able to access before, and that energy shows up for me in the language I find available to the poems. One of the primary distinctions between poetry and prose is the dividing of material into lines and stanzas. Poetry is an art of juxtaposition, and a poet's approach to arranging the content becomes one of the ways he or she develops a stylistic signature. I felt at one point too reliant upon a structure of twenty to twenty-four lines, usually in three stanzas that followed a pattern of conflict development and resolution, and in the pair of poems mentioned above, and many other recent poems, I have aspired to both the concision of a short poem and the expanse of a long poem.

One of the centerpiece works in *Tennessee Landscape* is a sequence of three related sonnets, under the title "Firing Order," that examines the rural life my family in upper East Tennessee has led for several generations and the cultural changes that have affected that way of being. The idea for this poem dates back at least a dozen years, as do a couple of other poems in the manuscript, though the final version that appears in the collection retains nothing of the first draft written then except for the central image of my father and me in a field working on an old truck. No other phrases or images from that short free verse poem contributed to the sonnet sequence in *Tennessee Landscape*, but that particular image held in my imagination for many years until I found the form that best accommodated it.

In a 1982 essay titled "The Origin of the Sonnet," Paul Oppenheimer proposes that modern poetry began when the sonnet form was discovered by the Italian poet of the early thirteenth century named Giacomo da Lentino. The sonnet form introduces a new potential for the lyric poem, an inward-searching poem not meant for public performance but intended for a private (or nonexistent) audience. Oppenheimer writes, "Giacomo's earliest sonnets themselves provide the strongest clues to the possibility that in writing them the poet was deliberately turning away from the kinds of songs made and sung by the troubadours and creating a new type of lyric with new, modern, and 'silent' intentions."[20] He believes that the importance of this development can hardly be overstated, as it forms for him the birth of the modern mind, an advance in the direction of meditation and self-reflection. It is, at the very least, a crucial step in the movement from Greek lyric to the English Renaissance and Shakespeare, and from there toward the greater Romantic lyric, which ultimately leads to the most consequential contemporary literature.

I have given a good deal of consideration to the ways in which one art form can interact with another. Several of the poems in *Tennessee Landscape* attempt to recreate episodes in which playing or listening to music

---

[20] Paul Oppenheimer, "The Origin of the Sonnet," in *The Birth of the Modern Mind: Self, Consciousness, and the Invention of the Sonnet* (New York: Oxford University Press, 1989), 297.

influences the scene or action, as in "Little Girl and the Dreadful Snake," "A Short Life of Trouble" (both take their titles from old folk-country ballads), and "Faubourg Marigny." The poem "Elemental Study" examines the way music and painting come together, as both try to articulate some internal struggle or passion, much the way poetry does. I have paid particular attention recently to how often-contrasted mediums such as poetry and painting might intersect. Ekphrastic poetry dates far back into the origins of poetry and exists in practically every age from the Greek lyric and Renaissance pastoral to the New York School poets of the 1950s. It is defined by James Heffernan simply as "the verbal representation of graphic representation." Ekphrasis in poetry provides both a means of interpretation and a stockpile of images through which the poet may examine an occurrence unrelated to the image in the visual artwork metaphorically, thus creating two levels of association for the poem's imagery.

Vincent Van Gogh's painting *The Night Café* struck me unexpectedly as I was scanning through the book *How to Read a Modern Painting*, looking for Arnold Bocklin's symbolist piece *Isle of the Dead*. The intensity of the image in *The Night Café*, a room depicted in low but stringent light, swirling and various shades of red and green, commanded my attention, and then the particulars of the scene began to evoke a vague familiarity, a sense of my own memories of such rooms. The larger idea occurred to me of how many hours I had spent in bars talking with friends, listening to music, and experiencing the full impact of their physical spaces, and I thought of the consequence of those times. Mostly, those moments were inconsequential, yet that also seemed significant. This line of thinking triggered a specific memory of time spent with a friend during the year I lived in New Orleans, and what our conversations had really been about, what they were really hoping to accomplish, and I began the poem "The Night Café, North Rendon, New Orleans." This poem appears just over a quarter of the way through *Tennessee Landscape with Blighted Pine* and employs the same long-line, unrhymed couplet structure as the earlier poems "Understory" and "Reading Late." I have generally used this structure to help balance episodes or sequences of the content that occur at more than one time in the past, though by no means in every poem in which that happens. This scene emerged over all the other instances in bars or restaurants that came to mind, I think because of what the speaker believes the two men are trying to accomplish—the preservation of their life experiences—in the exchange. The tone is wry at first but darkens as the conversation goes beyond shared musical interests and into the realm of personal failures, reflecting the mood of the painting and also the tendency for more private subject matter to arise after a conversation between friends continues. I believe this idea resonates with other poems based on significant moments within friendships, such "River Gods" (which precedes it in the book), "His Confession," and "Elemental Study."

I did not divide the poems in *Tennessee Landscape* into sections based on formal tendencies but rather tried to let resonances between individual poems determine the arrangement. For instance, a poem in received form, such as the pantoum "For the Frozen Wood," which begins the manuscript, carries within echoes of both theme and sentiment from the more experimental dropped-line form of "Tennessee Landscape with Blighted Pine," which opens the collection. Those poems benefit from being placed as bookends in the manuscript, and they have the opportunity to echo formal varieties and content-based similarities both forward and backward throughout the body of work. Most of the poems in *Tennessee Landscape* are written in open forms, and it is my hope that the significant number of poems written in traditional forms benefit from the juxtaposition.

I hope that the poems in *Tennessee Landscape*, and later collections, examine and exemplify not only theoretical concerns in modern and contemporary poetry but also the craft of shaping poems and the technique that brings them into being in the first place. Heaney writes about the difference between craft and technique in his essay "Feeling into Words," collected in his book *Preoccupations*, calling craft "the skill of making" but going much further with what technique means to a poet:

> Technique, as I would define it, involves not only a poet's way with words, his management of metre, rhythm, and verbal texture; it involves also a definition of his stance toward life, a definition of his own reality. It involves the discovery of ways to go beyond his normal cognitive bounds and raid the inarticulate: a dynamic alertness that mediates between the origins of feeling in memory and experience and the formal ploys that express these in a work of art.[21]

A poet must recognize truth and substance in his own voice, but I have been lucky to maintain a group of close and trusted readers, whether

---

[21] Heaney, "Feeling into Words," in *Preoccupations* (New York: FSG, 1980), 47.

in a university workshop, an informal set of friends, or a committee of professors working at the highest levels in the discipline, who have provided a second field of vision, another collection of eyes capable of recognizing inclinations, directions, influences, and wrong turnings in my work. The work in *Tennessee Landscape* represents my efforts to "raid the inarticulate," to use Heaney's echo of Eliot's "East Coker," and make poems out of the raw materials I have found there.

2

Gothic Realism in Appalachian Poetry[1]

Thank you to Emory & Henry College this afternoon for the opportunity to consider the relationship between Realism and the Gothic, and to explore two readerly and writerly approaches to the subject: one that looks backward to folklore and another that looks ahead to "lost futures." I intend to examine how these ideas have found a place in the works of Appalachian poets and writers, past and present, and where they might be going in the future, though admittedly these temporal frameworks are so intertwined that they can be hard to disentangle. Some of the traditional elements of Gothic literature are present in Appalachian writing: interactions with the wilderness, supernatural occurrences, and inexplicable violence. Appalachia does not have the ruined castles and abbeys or other ancient stone structures that inspired early British and German literary fascination with paganism and the Medieval, but those are replicated by the trace of Native American myths and rituals that remain as a buried layer in the culture. Certain hardships of the region, like poverty and geographic isolation, force a realistic rather than a fantastical look at those Gothic elements, so the idea of Gothic Realism resonates with the poetry, and the common lived experience, of Appalachia.

I tend to think about modes like the Gothic and realism by how they

---

[1] Presented at Emory & Henry College, October 24, 2019.

are implemented into poems and stories from a creative writer's perspective and from a teacher's point of view. Most of the prompts I use for poetry workshops, and most of my own poems, examine the world as we know it. I have written prompts that explore many of the elements of lived experience, such as family history, natural environments, the particular *inscape* of certain objects, and gifts given and received. I have always thought of Walt Whitman's "I Am the Poet of Reality" as something like a poet's job description: we go down into the earth, into the past, and into the details of life, we "reconnoitre" there, and we come back with a report of what we found. There exists, however, a whole realm of experience that does not fit cleanly into the category of realism. Some of the richest cultural traditions are based not on historical facts but on folklore, which may or may not be rooted in actual occurrences. I think it is important to remember the mythic origins of literature and the role that local, even family, mythology plays in the development of a writer's imagination. I have always wished that I could write a poem that felt at once as equally real and unreal as Robert Frost's "The Witch of Coös." Lore makes room for the unexplained, and the most memorable poems often retain some sense of mystery about them.

In a writing prompt, I ask students to consider a folkloric story, preferably a tale recalled from their childhood, and recast it, without judgment or explanation, in a relatively short narrative poem. I leave formal elements open for this assignment, though I have found that syllabic patterns, even rhyme schemes, can help give shape and structure to poems that rely heavily on narrative techniques. I remind students that folklore takes many shapes and that urban legends and contemporary mysteries are just as much a part of the unwritten literature of a people and place as very old tales. Possibly the most famous American poem, Edgar Allan Poe's "The Raven," is steeped in mythology and lore, so most students will be familiar with some version of this approach to poetry. Some of the most famous British poems also operate in a Gothic vein, like "The Rime of the Ancient Mariner" by Samuel Taylor Coleridge, "Goblin Market" by Christina Rosetti, and most of the dramatic monologues by Robert Browning, like "Soliloquy of the Spanish Cloister" and "My Last Duchess." A reader and writer can generally find a lineage of Gothic poetry to connect to their imaginations and experiences. My hope is that students will see in their own writing some trace of familiar favorites and will branch out from there to find threads of literature and philosophy that they have not yet discovered, and that by such route new doors may be opened.

The term "hauntology" was coined by the French philosopher Jacques Derrida in his 1993 book *Spectres of Marx*, a book he opens with an epigraph from *Hamlet*: "Time is out of joint." "Hauntology" is a portmanteau word, which blends two words and two definitions into one. "Haunt" of course is familiar to us, and in one Merriam-Webster definition it is defined as "to visit or inhabit as a ghost." Haunt is combined with the philosophical concept of "ontology," which means "the study of being." Derrida says there is a "logic of haunting" that addresses the meaning of returning images and ideas from the past along with matters of death, judgment, and the final destiny for the soul. Derrida essentially says that we perceive the present only in relation to the past and can only picture the future as an altered version of the past. The present, therefore, is always intertwined with the past and the imagined future.

I first discovered this term "hauntology" in British music writer Mark Fisher's book *The Weird and the Eerie*—and was fascinated with how these ideas emerge in literature, film, and music. For instance, he says, "the eerie is when there is something where there should be nothing, and nothing where there should be something." Fisher maintained an influential blog in the early 2000s under the name "K-Punk" and wrote about "retro-futurism" in recording artists like Amy Winehouse and Artic Monkeys, near-exact replicas of early genres of music but with modern production. Fisher criticizes this approach while recognizing its obvious pleasures. His concern is that the new art too closely replicates the old art we once loved without creating any new understanding of the past in which that art was produced, or without making room for new art in the present. Such a concept resonates with Appalachian literature, which appears more invested than other contemporary writing in making a record of the past before it is lost.

In my view, the quintessential Appalachian folklore poem is Robert Morgan's "Mountain Bride." That poem presents a folktale told as a true story, and it may well have been one at some point or based on one.

Mountain Bride

They say Revis found a flatrock
on the ridge just

perfect for a natural hearth,
and built his cabin with a stick
and clay chimney right over it.
On their wedding night he lit
the fireplace to dry away the mountain
chill of late spring and flung on
applewood to dye
the room with molten color while
he and Martha that was a Parrish
warmed the sheets between the tick
stuffed with leaves and its feather
cover. Under that wide hearth
a nest of rattlers,
they'll knot a hundred together,
had wintered and were coming awake.
The warming rock
flushed them out early.
It was she
who wakened to their singing near
the embers and roused him to go look.
Before he reached the fire
more than a dozen struck
and he died yelling her to stay
on the big four-poster.
Her uncle coming up the hollow
with a gift bearham two days later
found her shivering there
marooned above a pool
of hungry snakes,
and the body beginning to swell.

Morgan's poem has many of the elements of what we could call "frontier gothic," which often depicts the vulnerabilities of humans in the wilderness, and how Nature can be a malevolent force. Irony is a common feature of the Gothic, saying one thing and another, generally its opposite, as when the rattling of the snakes' tails is referred to as "singing." The horror is that the young wife can't even escape the scene after her husband has died right before her eyes but must wait two days(!) alone in her marriage bed for rescue. Morgan once shared an experience of meeting a reader who wondered if he had borrowed the tale from John Ehle's 1964 novel *The Landbreakers*. Morgan had not read the novel before writing his poem but thought the story had happened to someone his grandfather had known personally in the mountains of western North Carolina. To me, this illustrates the nature of lore—it may exist in many different forms and be told and retold, revised and rearranged, in many different places, each time with some sense of both the local and the universal.

I looked back through some of the major early Appalachian poets, such as James Still and Emma Bell Miles, and I found examples of supernatural happenings, mostly in a folkloric context, examples of extreme violence, and other elements of the Gothic. One of the most direct examples I found was by the continually overlooked East Tennessee poet George Scarbrough, in his poem "Still Life: Dead Mule." Scarbrough wrote often of the horrors of a childhood in extreme poverty, with a violent and illiterate father who felt threatened by his son's intellect and book learning. Here are the opening lines of the poem:

> In the gothic underglow
> Of elder woods, we found him so:
> Against the thread moss of whose miter
> Like matches burned around him, lighter
> Than the purple leaves, he lay
> Aboiling on that dullard day:
> Himself the structural paradigm
> Of what was true of us and him.

Scarbrough's speaker finds the mule's body and sees it as an emblem for the lives of struggle and decay his family leads. Scarbrough situates the "elder woods" as the site of Gothic horror and reality, where the mule is found in a grotesque state of decay. Later in the poem, the speaker says of the image, "Great sights so break the mind in two," summoning both the terror and beauty long associated with the sublime.

The presence of the weird and the eerie have played a role in my own imagination, and I have tried to make room for the unexplained in my poems. William Wright and I published a book called *Specter Mountain* that attempts to invent a place whose culture would be very definitely Appalachia but is not limited to the historical facts of one specific location and landscape. Wright and I certainly had elements of the Gothic in mind with that project; even before the poems were composed, we were thinking of some of the ghost stories about Roan Mountain in Tennessee and also about the Brocken Spectre images from the Harz Mountains of Germany. But we didn't want to write only about literal ghosts—we also intended to examine the spectral afterlives of mountaintop removal coal mining and the residue of meth labs seeping into streams and creeks. We needed to incorporate the future consequences of past actions into the landscape.

Rather than engage more with that volume, I would rather introduce a theme from Wright's own work. Lyricism is the primary mode in Wright's poetry, but many of his poems are driven by characters and their narratives. The selections from his book-length poem *Bledsoe* give the deepest immersion into a fictional world where disability and strained family ties bleed into a kind of violence normally associated with true crime drama. In later poems, like "The Milk Witch," from *Tree Heresies*, Wright moves beyond folklore into the realm of folk horror, a genre more often discussed in studies of films like *The Wicker Man*, *Children of the Corn*, and the recent *Midsommar* than in literature. The image of "the season's rain / locked behind her smiling eyes" reminds us why we fear what happens in the dark and why we suspect unnatural forces at work when crops fail and cows run dry. Anyone who reads of the furrow plowed by the blonde mare, or of the shrouded conjuring of the milk witch, will recognize the fine and distinctive thread of the Gothic in William Wright's very contemporary poetry.

Appalachian writers of all genres have explored the Gothic, especially in the way the past intrudes upon the present. The Knoxville-born horror and dark fantasy writer Karl Edward Wagner spoke in a 1981 interview about the Gothic as a definitive form of horror writing. In his own writings, Wagner employed realistic people and places, the world as we recognize it, as the setting for manifestations of the Gothic imagination. Some of his most successful stories, such as "In the Pines" and ".220 Swift," take place in Appalachia and engage with the environment and folklore of the region. Wagner coined the term "Acid Gothic," somewhat tongue-in-cheek, to describe his modernization of traditional material of cosmic horror, such as the survival of liches, ancient cults, and lost civilizations. It may not be a coincidence that the book that Mark Fisher was writing at the time of his death was to be titled *Acid Communism*. Fisher looked back from the 2010s to Wagner's era of the late 1960s and '70s as a moment when authentic cultural exploration thrived and new futures could be imagined. It may only be coincidence that Wagner's final published story, a tie-in with British fantasist Michael Moorcock's Multiverse, was titled "The Gothic Touch."

The subject of mourning for lost futures is especially poignant and concrete in the example of the opioid epidemic in Appalachia, which extends backward a bit to the now hardly mentioned meth craze of just a few years back and the still not fully acknowledged wave of heroin use in the region. There are literal "lost futures" in the lives cut short, often in youth, by drug use and the lives of the children left behind, even if they are lucky enough to be living with grandparents or in caring foster homes. Current lawsuits holding Big Pharma responsible for the crisis represent huge gains for the people affected but also risk oversimplifying the fabric of responsibility, focusing only on the richest and least personal of the many parties involved. These often include friends, family members, and well-meaning doctors but also an economy in which finding meaningful, sustaining, and living-wage work is exceedingly difficult in some places. This resonates with Fisher's idea of "Capitalist Realism," and another term he occasionally used for this experience is "retro-futurism"—the continual recreation of an imaginary future that did not happen but was envisioned at some point in the past that we look back on as more hopeful or filled with possibility.

This concept is both cultural and political in the sense that capitalist neo-liberalism is interested in the free market, and whatever does not thrive there is in constant danger of being lost or outmoded. If a demand exists for dangerous or destructive products, they are certain to be produced and delivered one way or another, legally or not. In a look backward to the 1970s, we can read Marilou Awiakta's poems about nuclear anxiety and about the contrast between modern times and the Cherokee ways of life of her ancestors. In a look forward, we can begin to see this anxiety in poems about the Anthropocene—like my panel mate Jessica Cory's new anthology of Appalachian nature writing. In William Brewer's recent book, *I Know Your Kind*, we hear poems in the voices of drug addicts and their family members whose lives have been destroyed. Appalachian writing has looked at the Gothic horrors of drug use and other scenes of cultural destruction, like mountaintop removal and racial and class-based economic disparity.

One of the most fascinating aspects of hauntology is the universality of nostalgia for futures that have been cancelled, and how the nostalgia crosses political, and religious, barriers. Progressives feel that the ghosts of possible futures are lurking because the conservatives won't let the past die and the future be born. Conservatives feel that the best times are behind us, and we better grab hold of all we can while we can—Brexit and "Make America Great Again" are certainly examples of people grasping for a version of the past in lieu of possible futures that they dread. At the heart of this matter is a simple question: "What might have been?" This query has been around forever, in poetry and in culture, in Appalachia and across the world, and the answers to it are always as much about the future as they are about the past.

Works Cited

Derrida, Jacques. *Specters of Marx*. New York: Routledge, 1994.

Fisher, Mark. *The Weird and the Eerie*. London: Revolver Press, 2015.

Graves, Jesse. "Lore." *Piano in a Sycamore: Writing Exercises from the Appalachian Writers' Workshop*, ed. Silas House and Marianne Worthington. Hindman Settlement School, 2017.

Morgan, Robert. "Mountain Bride." *The Strange Attractor: New and Selected Poems*. Baton Rouge: LSU Press, 2004.

Scarbrough, George. "Still Life: Dead Mule." *New and Selected Poems*. Binghamton, NY: Iris Press, 1977.

Wagner, Karl Edward. "Interview with Dr. Jeffrey Elliot." *Fantasy Newsletter*. July 1981.

Wright, William. "The Milk Witch." *Tree Heresies*. Macon, GA: Mercer University Press, 2015.

3

Tennessee Said-Song:
Dialect in Appalachian Poetry

In his important essay on poetry and experience, "Feeling into Words," the Nobel Prize-winning Irish poet Seamus Heaney considers an intriguing device used in an Aleksandr Solzhenitsyn novel: "The idea was that a voice is like a fingerprint, possessing a constant and unique signature, and like a fingerprint, can be recorded and employed for identification."[1] The device in question is a decoder that can identify a speaker despite his trying to mask his voice, and though the device is fictional, its implications resonate when considering how an individual's genetic code determines that person's means of communication. Heaney goes on to discuss the manner by which a poet comes to find his or her own "voice," meaning in this case not simply a speaking instrument that all humans are born with but rather the complex blend of lexicon, intonation, level of diction, variety of syntax, and palette of images that a poet employs to represent a particular vision of the world. For Heaney, this is not simply a matter of literary influence or taste, though a poet's voice certainly can be modified and refined through cultivation and exposure to new or attractive means of artistic expression. Primarily, however, voice is something that develops before reading skills or language acquisition and is in large part preconscious—if

---

[1] Seamus Heaney, "Feeling into Words," in *Preoccupations: Selected Prose, 1968–1978* (New York: FSG, 1980), 43.

we are not born "with" it, we are at least born "into" it.

One might suggest that there is a Romantic and counter-scientific element to Heaney's version of poetic voice, and it may sound like a remnant of the pre-Darwinian era, but few poets are willing to attribute the entirety of their calling, or gift, or sensibility at the very minimum, to the random entanglements of brain chemistry or neuron connectivity. As a frequent writer in the English language, and as a poet in particular, I am concerned with the role one's dialect, or local accent, plays in a writer's finding of his or her own singular voice, and this is an especially pressing subject for me, as I have retained very little of the accent of my home community. In my particular case, the "fingerprint" of the dialect I heard spoken during my entire childhood, a distinct version of Southern Appalachian rural speech, is far removed from the formal and elevated language of poetry and academic criticism in which I now work as an English professor.

I grew up in an age of emerging media, of technological innovation, and of rapid suburban expansion, though in the remote farming community of Sharps Chapel, Tennessee, those developments hardly touched most in the community. It might be useful to give a sense of what type of place Sharps Chapel was before the 1970s and to illustrate the speech as it might have been heard at the time. I would also like to draw some conclusions as to why I did not carry on with the accent of my closest family members, what determinations I made in acquiring my own approach to language, and whether cultural influences made significant impact on my decision, conscious or unconscious, to lose the most distinctive features of my home dialect.

The history of my family in Sharps Chapel mirrors in some ways the history of the place and tells a story of westward migration, made by immigrants looking for independence more than for prosperity. The community lies about thirty miles south of Cumberland Gap, made famous by Daniel Boone as the trail he carved out on his explorations, and thought of at the time as the "gateway to the west." The landscape of Sharps Chapel is a bit less rugged than Cumberland Gap, flatter with more viable farmland, though the ground is given to sinkholes and hot water springs. Before the construction of Norris Dam by the Tennessee Valley Authority (TVA), two rivers, the Clinch and the Powell, converged to become a tributary of the larger, swifter Tennessee River. It formed an ideal stopping point for westward travelers looking for farmland, and my ancestors, John and Peter Graves, along with their ninety-year-old father, Johannes Graff, came with their sister and her husband, Henry Scharp, to settle along the river banks in what is now Sharps Chapel. John Graves came to the area from Orange County (now Alamance County), North Carolina, and cleared six hundred acres of river-bottom land to farm and set up a timber trade. He brought the rest of his family over, and they started a business floating log rafts downstream as far as Chattanooga. John's father, Johannes Graff, was born in 1703 in the German Palatinate and sailed from Rotterdam in 1730, from which he eventually arrived in Berks County, Pennsylvania. He died in Sharps Chapel in 1804, though his grave marker was lost in the TVA cemetery removals.

My family has lived in and around Sharps Chapel since the first arrivals in the 1780s; my parents continue to live there, and my older sister has raised her children there. The speech pattern of lifetime residents resembles the model presented by Cratis D. Williams in his excellent study, *Southern Mountain Speech*. In one representative example, a speaker of the rural Appalachian dialect of East Tennessee tends toward a strong *R* sound at the ends of words. For instance, a Sharps Chapel native might say "backer" for tobacco, rather than the cartoonish "te-backee" of popular imitations of the Southern accent. Similarly, "window" becomes "winder" and "potato" becomes "tater," and an ending *Y* sound is often added to words like "idea," which becomes "idy," as in, "I ain't got no idy whur she is." And, on occasion, an internal *R* appears in words such as "rurn" for "ruin," or "breakferst" for "breakfast." Williams attributes these characteristics to the heavy Scots-Irish influence in the region, and though my ancestors were German, they must have assimilated some of the accent of the majority population in the places they lived and traded. To illustrate the sounds in action, Williams translates a passage from the folktale "The Fox and the Bum'lebee" as follows: "Oncet thay uz a fox 'at tuck a notion one mornin' he'd walk daown to the store in the settlemints at the maouth of the creek."[2] These sounds are familiar to me, though they sound more like the oldest of my relatives from childhood, and I don't know anyone today who speaks in quite so drawn-out a way. For instance, "oncet" remains current to my ear, and so does "thay" for "there," but Williams's example of "daown" sounds as foreign to me as "te-backee."

[2] Cratis D. Williams, *Southern Mountain Speech* (Berea: Berea College Press, 1992), 5.

At a later point in his essay, "Feeling into Words," Heaney quotes some witty lines from the poem "The Character of Ireland" by the late Irish poet W.R. Rodgers:

An abrupt people
Who like the spiky consonants of speech
And think the soft ones cissy; who dig
The k and t in orchestra, detect sin
In *sinfonia*, get a kick out of
Tin-cans, fricatives, fornication, staccato talk,
Anything that gives or takes attack,
Like Micks, Teagues, tinker's gets, Vatican.[3]

Here I begin to see the contrast between Heaney's reverence for his native dialect and my insecurity about my own. An Irish accent, in broad terms, has both a literary cache and a hard-knocks validity, and it comes with certain cultural representatives, the best of which being the giant figure of Yeats and least of which being the stereotype of the drunken barfighter, not the worst of associations for the impassioned life of a poet. My dialectal signature, however, is most popularly represented in the figures of Jed Clampett and Gomer Pyle, hapless bumpkins from 1960s-era television programs, and in literature most often connected with William Faulkner's Snopes family, Erskine Caldwell's tenant farmers, or Flannery O'Connor's many "poor white trash" characters. Even before I knew I wanted to be a writer and a teacher, I knew that I did not want to sound like Jed Clampett, though I also recognized the difference in even the most colorful of country talk—my mother was given to odd colloquialisms and unexpected word combinations—and the Hollywood version of "hillbilly" parody.

At age seven, for instance, I would not have been in a cultural position to decide that I needed to drop certain sounds and figures from the way my family spoke, and the same would be true even at age twelve or fifteen. I had never met a college professor until I arrived for my first college classes at Lincoln Memorial University in Harrogate, Tennessee, in fall 1991. I did not imagine from childhood that I might have wanted to be a college professor, because I had nothing on which to base such an idea, much less

---

[3] W. R. Rodgers, quoted in Heaney, "Feeling into Words," 44–45.

the manner of speaking it might have required. Yet as early as I can remember, people commented on the way I spoke, especially when I met them for the first time. I was an early reader, and my mother—who, had she received some guidance in literature, might have chosen a life similar to mine—read to me often, so I had access to expanded vocabulary, and though we had only two television stations, I still heard a good deal of the unaccented speech, in the mode of Tom Brokaw, generally preferred on television programs.

In the case of my own writing, I have held on to the images and occurrences of my childhood, details of landscape and evocations of individuals, more closely than to the sounds of speech. Many of my poems document not only my experiences and memories but also those of past generations of my family. It was my great fortune to have the opportunity to study as a Master of Fine Arts student, in poetry writing, at Cornell University with two of the most accomplished Southern poets of the twentieth century, the late A. R. Ammons and Robert Morgan. Both Ammons and Morgan grew up in North Carolina, Ammons in the eastern flatlands and Morgan in the state's western mountains, less than a hundred miles from the Tennessee border. They both also grew up in the kind of rural poverty and isolation familiar to my childhood and have each written beautifully, and distinctly, about the way of life of their own particular homeplaces. I learned a great deal from each poet on writing about one's place and have generally agreed with Morgan's caution about the risk of a reader's not taking poetry seriously that contains too much dialect speech; and like Morgan, I prefer to represent the culture of my people through objects and stories. Nevertheless, I find an irresistible music in A. R. Ammons's "Carolina Said-Songs," the first of which contains these lines:

In them days
they won't hardly no way to know if
  somebody way off
died
    till they'd be
    dead and buried

       and Uncle Jim

hitched up a team of mules to the wagon

and he cracked the whip over them
and run them their dead-level best
the whole thirty miles to your great grandma's funeral
down there in
Green Sea County[4]

The poem goes on to tell the story of a thunderstorm and runaway mules, and it includes the epigraph, "*(as told to me by an aunt)*." My feeling is that the events of this story could be retold effectively by any storyteller, but the *poetry*, the "voice," as Heaney calls it, emanates from the music of the aunt's verbal presence. The poem gains a "firsthand" quality to it that comes both from the aunt's being there to witness the occurrence and from the poet's being there to witness his aunt's telling of it. The poem becomes an art-tribute to the aunt's voice as much as to the story she tells. A cynic might suggest that we receive not an authentic version of the aunt's story but a poet's romantic vision of an aunt's story; however, we do not ask literature to suspend perspective, and we do not hold it to the word-for-word account of journalistic quotation. In other words, we accept it as poetry and believe in the testimony that poetry gives.

In my own poetry, I have only once tried to replicate the native speech of Sharps Chapel through the recording of dialogue, and my sense is that I achieved mixed results. The occasion for the poem, however, seemed to require the most truthful and accurate representation I could give it. An elderly neighbor of my parents, Clytus Campbell, who has since passed away, agreed to drive with my father and me down to the banks of Norris Lake, which he remembered from his boyhood as the Clinch riverbanks. We had asked him to tell us anything he could remember of what the community looked like, and he surprised us both with the precision and vitality of his recollections. I knew that I had to write about it—it had been my selfish hope all along—and I knew that to try to present Clytus's voice in the words and sounds of my voice would not capture the full range of his story, which to me was contained in his way of telling as much as in the content of what he told us. These are the opening two and half stanzas from the poem "The Sunken Mill," as it was published in *CrossRoads: A Southern Culture Annual, 2006*:

---

[4] A. R. Ammons, "Carolina Said-Songs," in *Collected Poems, 1951–1971* (New York: Norton, 2001), 55.

A nest of trees across the lake,
taller in their crowns than the treeline,
too far from our shore to make out
a leafshape or trace a pattern over the bark.

Just below them trees about twenty feet,
he said, showing with two extended fingers
angled in their joints as a hammer claw,
was your people's grist mill.

The old feller was blind, and that's what they
called him, Blind Graves. I never knowed
any other name for him...

    I include lines from the poem as both evidential conclusion and coda to my study of the speech of Sharps Chapel, Tennessee, and though I have not retained all of its characteristics in the way I communicate with the world, I hope that I may still be able to represent it as it has shaped the voice that became my own.

PART 2

4

Awake in Their Wide Pasture:
Formal Design in the Poems of Robert Morgan and Ron Rash

Ron Rash and Robert Morgan are widely known as writers of narratives—of novels, poems, and short stories that invest deeply in the voices and experiences of characters. Both writers work with themes that are specific to the culture of Appalachia, and both have used their home region almost exclusively as the setting for their works. They imbue their native landscapes with a lyrical beauty, while never looking away from the hardships of life in remote and sometimes backward places. Embracing literary forms is a deeply personal choice for a writer, not unlike the choice to represent a region or way of life. Inherent abilities and tendencies, such as the kind of perfect-pitch ear for meter that some poets appear to possess, can account for significant influence in the engagement with formal techniques. An affinity with tradition, however, or an interest in the past that goes beyond what happened and into the shape those happenings assumed, can also determine the modes and measures with which the poet elects to work. Poetic form is a part of literary history and also a part of cultural history, and many writers have viewed it as one of the beauties of nature, and of human accomplishment, and as part of the inheritance of any poet. For Ron Rash and Robert Morgan, their choices of form have involved employing tradition with variation. They have sought an adaptable form, a means that is at home both in the culture they represent in their work and with the long traditions of poetic composition.

Since the publication in 1969 of Robert Morgan's first book of poetry, *Zirconia Poems*, and Fred Chappell's earliest collection of poems, *The World between the Eyes*, in 1971, the genre of "Appalachian Poetry" has experienced a renaissance unique in its history. Soon to follow were first full-length books by Jeff Daniel Marion and George Ella Lyon, and then within another decade, early books by Maggie Anderson, Katherine Stripling Byer, and Michael McFee would help to carve out a significant corner of American poetry for a group of voices distinct from "Southern Literature" at large, finding its roots and subject matter in the Southern mountains. Formally, however, there was great diversity within this group of poets, with Morgan and Marion electing to write in the spare, often short-lined free verse driven by closely examined images and landscapes, whereas Chappell put a variety of forms and rhyme schemes to use, often to highlight his caustic wit and narrative sensibility. Increasingly, Appalachian poets have moved toward formal designs in their work, particularly including the more frequent usage of syllabic verse (the controlled repetition of syllable counts within individual poetic lines, unaccompanied by metrical or rhyme patterns), which suggests an interesting case study as to the goals and outcomes of these recent formal directions.[1] Perhaps the only Appalachian poet who has been as widely regarded as Morgan and Rash over the past decade is Charles Wright, who has written, "In poems, all concerns are concerns of form."[2] The poems of Robert Morgan and Ron Rash present illustrative examples of why syllabics and other tendencies toward form have become important elements in the poetry of Appalachia, and also serve as models by which to examine the impact of this movement.

---

[1] A notable example of this trend toward formal design among Appalachian poets can be found in Yale Younger Poet's Prize-winner Maurice Manning's 2007 collection *Bucolics*, which employs a consistent syllabic structure throughout. Manning measures the voice of a farm worker speaking in heavy rural dialect into regular syllabic lines, all the while maintaining the naturalness of the narrator's speech.

[2] Charles Wright was born in Tennessee in 1935 and taught for many years at the University of Virginia. He has been named United States Poet Laureate, won the Pulitzer Prize and the National Book Award, and is generally considered a strong candidate for the permanent canon of American poetry.

Less than a decade separates Rash and Morgan in age, but Rash's first volume of poems, *Eureka Mill*, appeared in 2000, while Morgan's first book, *Zirconia Poems*, came out in 1969, placing a full generation of readers between those debut books. One might call Ron Rash a member of the "Second Wave" of the Appalachian Literary Renaissance, because the surge that began in 1972 has not declined even momentarily in the thirty-five years since but has simply been followed by a younger group of writers of potentially equal ability. The two writers share a number of qualities beyond their usage of formal poetic devices; both grew up among extended family in the western Carolinas (North for Morgan, North and South for Rash), and they come from families that survived on rural farm work as well as labor in cotton mill towns. Both are better known as fiction writers, publishing novels and short story collections, though each first gained wide recognition for their poetry. The precedent for multi-genre Appalachian writers traces back to the first generation of Southern mountain poets who earned a national readership, including Jesse Stuart and James Still, both accomplished poets who are best remembered for their fiction. Morgan and Rash are also both narrative poets who rely on one of the cornerstones of the lyric mode, an unswerving attention to the minutiae of particular moments in time to center the emotional resonance of their work.

Another common trait is that neither poet began his career writing syllabic verse. Robert Morgan's first three books, *Zirconia Poems*, the chapbook *Life in the Crosshairs*, and *Red Owl*, present poems of such compressed lucidity that they seem to have been formed by underground pressures exactly as were the zircons dug from mines in Morgan's native Henderson County, North Carolina. Morgan's early poems were spare, tight, and primarily concerned with embodying the object in their crosshairs. In an unexpected turn, as Morgan's poems became more conversational, more about people and their stories, they also assumed more regular formal designs, countering the standard claim that free verse closely resembles spoken language. Conversely, Ron Rash began his career as a poet writing sustained narratives, as in his first book of poems, *Eureka Mill*. That collection tells about the lives the speaker's grandparents lived in a cotton mill town, and like Morgan, Rash is attuned to the details of natural environments and interior spaces in these early poems.

Among the several aesthetic reasons that two poets as remarkably gifted as Robert Morgan and Ron Rash would move toward formal structures in their poems, two motives emerge most convincingly. First, both poets are invested in creating a sense of the living past, what Morgan has called "a community across time."[3] Part of the living past of poetry is structural and aural regularity, the continuity of sound patterns and visual recognitions, that creates a bond and an agreement between the poet and the reader. In their recent work, Morgan and Rash fill the worlds of their poems with voices of long distant ancestors, memories of departed family members, and stories and myths from their home communities. Like so many Appalachian poets, Morgan and Rash strive to evoke the sense of a continuous merging of past and present within worldly experience, while also establishing a note of particularity, a unique perspective through the pitch of their own poetic voices. This relates to the second compelling reason for a shift to more regular forms, which is to take a stance against prevailing cultural trends. American poetry since the 1960s has witnessed the rise of Beat poetry; the New York School and its stars, Frank O'Hara and John Ashbery; the Black Arts Movement; the Black Mountain School; "Disembodied Poetics"; Language poetry; and what Tony Hoagland has recently called "the skittery poem of our moment."[4] Each of these movements takes a radical position in regard to verse form, all in favor of open forms.

In lyric poetry, a mastery of forms is secondary to the resonance of content, and it is notable that both Morgan and Rash also write poems without syllable patterns, in standard free verse, and in other, often more complicated verse forms. In one of his signature poems, "Honey," from the 2000 collection *Topsoil Road*, Morgan revisits the image of the lattice[5] as a term of design, in this case to describe the hives of honey bees:

> a sealed relic of sun and time
> and roots of many acres fixed
> in crystal-tight arrays, in rows

---

[3] Robert Morgan has used this phrase in interviews, including on *The Oprah Winfrey Show*, but I first heard it when he visited a class I was teaching at Cornell, and the phrase so resonated with my students that several included it in their final papers.

[4] Tony Hoagland's essay, "Fear of Narrative and the Skittery Poem of Our Moment," a critique of the state of contemporary American poetry, first appeared in *Poetry* in March 2006.

[5] Morgan also used this term in his prose piece, "Mica: Reflective Bits from Notebooks."

and lattices of sweeter latin
from scattered prose of meadow, woods.

The first definition of "lattice" in *The American Heritage Dictionary* reflects the most familiar building-trade terminology: "An open framework made of strips of metal, wood, or similar material interwoven to form regular, patterned spaces." This is fitting as an image for the effect of writing syllabic lines, but there is also a third dictionary entry that applies to physics (a field Morgan has studied carefully and whose language he has brought to his poetry): "A regular, periodic configuration of points, particles, or objects throughout an area of space, especially the arrangement of ions or molecules in a crystalline solid." This breaking down of the line into its smallest particles deepens the metaphor of poetry as latticework, without losing the freedom of the "open framework" so necessary to the poetics of Morgan and Rash. The pitfalls of working exclusively with a single syllabic count include the risk of sameness and predetermination, of limiting experience to representation on an artificially limited canvas, so Morgan and Rash create frameworks for their poems with many different materials and textures.

The earliest instance of the eight-syllable line pattern in Robert Morgan's work appears in his 1987 collection *At the Edge of the Orchard Country*, strikingly in the poem "Lightning Bug" and subtly in several others. The opening lines of many of the book's most memorable poems, such as "Buffalo Trace," "Yellow," "The Gift of Tongues," and "Man and Machine," introduce the pattern but do not employ it throughout. Though lines such as "Sometimes in the winter mountains" and "The whole church got hot and vivid" are not metrically consistent, Morgan establishes a definite visual and aural echo effect that surfaces and resurfaces through the entire book, like a thread woven into an intricate design, barely visible in the fabric of the whole. In the poem "Lightning Bug," we see the emergence of the model Morgan would use more frequently in later work, in which the eight-syllable line is used for the whole poem. The content of "Lightning Bug," however, harks back to Morgan's earliest "object" poems, with its close study of a thing existing in its element—a living thing in this case, though it is given the grandeur of permanence in the poem's beautiful opening line:

Carat of the first radiance.
You navigate like a creature
of the deep. I wish I could read
your morse across the night yard.
Your body is a piece of star
but your head is obscure. What small
photography! What instrument
panel is on? You are winnowed
through the hanging gardens of night.
Your noctilucent syllables
sing in the millennium of
the southern night with star-talking
dew, like the thinker sending nous
into the outerstillness from
the edge of the orchard country.

An unassuming poem about one of the most common mysteries of summer, the luminescence of nocturnal flying insects, hardly nominates itself as a pivotal work, but it is perfectly characteristic of Robert Morgan's method to submerge a crucial formal shift, the broad influence of which is still felt, within a poem about a humble subject. Morgan has noted that he began writing this poem in 1969[6] but was unable to complete it until he came upon the poem's concluding line, from which the collection takes its title and which may have suggested the poem's rhythm.

Morgan mentions the syllabic form as early as his 1983 essay "Good Measure," as it applies to the poem "Grandma's Bureau."[7] Morgan says,

"Grandma's Bureau" represents much of the work I have been doing recently. The versification is the simplest I know, an eight-syllable line with no regular meter, no counting of stresses. It is almost-free

---

[6] In his essay, "The Cubist of Memory," Morgan says, "Finally the phrase…came to me this year (1983). It suggested redolence, proximity and distance, a projecting of attention out to the horizon of trees and stars. Suddenly the poem felt complete, and I could let it rest" (in *Good Measure*, 11).

[7] The poem mentioned, "Grandma's Bureau," was collected later in the 1990 volume *Sigodlin*, though it was not re-collected in either *Green River* (1991) or *The Strange Attractor* (2004), Morgan's two "New and Selected" volumes.

verse broken into an arbitrary length, based vaguely on four-beat common meter: a kind of humble blank verse. I like this form because it leaves the musical cadence almost entirely free to follow the content, the narrative line, the local dynamics of the sentence, yet has some of the surface tension of regularity, the expectation of repetition, with the fulfillment and surprises of advancement across an uneven terrain.[8]

By the time of his 1990 collection, *Sigodlin,* Morgan had begun to work more rigorously with verse forms, including a highly successful pantoum ("Audubon's Flute") and an equally striking anagram poem ("Mountain Graveyard"), as well as a number of poems with the eight-syllable line. In *Topsoil Road,* Morgan's most recent collection of all-new work, the majority of poems use the eight-syllable line. Some of Morgan's most memorable poems appear in this volume, including "Topsoil Road," "Wild Peavines," "History's Madrigal," and two poems on the poet's father, "Mowing" and "Working in the Rain." "Mowing" presents an especially interesting case because we see Morgan taking on one of his central subjects, the nature of his father, and breaking with his signature syllabic form in doing so. A looser, more expansive line emerges, almost Whitmanesque, such as "Half-dancing and half-rowing into a weed bank" and "a wide wing of metal, tempered in Czechoslovakia." In a book filled with controlled line lengths and regular syllable counts, the freedom these lines offer leaps off the page with the energy of the work they represent. They achieve the best kind of mimetic effect, in which the form becomes a natural extension of its subject matter.

In his two most recent collections, *Terroir* (2011) and *Dark Energy* (2014), Robert Morgan has continued his work with the eight-syllable line, but in many poems, he has also introduced a new formal development: the rhyming end couplet. The effect creates a dramatic sense of closure and offers an unexpected pleasure when no other rhymes have been established earlier in the poem. Take for instance the effect at the end of "October Crossing," a poem about "woolly bear" caterpillars, from the collection *Terroir*:

However accurate the widths
of colors on their prophet backs,

---

[8] In *Good Measure,* 6.

or knowledge of their fate as moths,
they seem intent on crossing this
hard Styx or Jordan to the ditch,
oblivious to the tires' high pitch. (lines 8–13)

The conclusion of the poem, with its "ditch/pitch" end rhyme, elevates the seemingly unremarkable journey of the caterpillar to significant drama, a life-or-death situation. These caterpillars already have a cultural mythology associated with their appearance; they are supposed to predict the duration of winter by the width of the orange stripes on their backs, and in some Appalachian communities, it is considered bad luck for the caterpillars to see one's teeth.

Morgan employs the end rhyme in well over half of the poems in *Terroir* and in a similar number in *Dark Energy*, though the device hardly appears at all in his earlier work. Regarding the new technique, Morgan says, "I'm sure it was Shakespeare's use of the tag couplet in many of his soliloquies that inspired me to try tying off a poem with a rhyme."[9] In *Dark Energy*, Morgan uses an addendum to the end rhyme with what could be considered a concept-rhyme, as in the conclusion of the poem "Widdershins," in which the final two lines end with the words "said" and "heard." The conceptual association between "said" and "heard" makes a kind of logical sense, even a kind of grammatical sense, as between verb and object. While the alliterative "d" that ends each word could make a case for these words as a slant-rhyme, another example from the title poem, "Dark Energy," which concludes with lines ending in "zero" and "silence," shows a clear relation between the meanings of the words. In Morgan's concept-rhymes, one end word answers the other and provides a context for interpreting the other. Such poem endings include "birth" and "work" in "Big Talk," and "particles" and "fine rain" in "Rare." Almost all of Morgan's newer poems maintain the eight-syllable line, his "humble blank verse," while introducing further formal inventions.

Ron Rash favors a tighter, more dramatic syllabic line than Robert Morgan, working often with only seven syllables per line, calling back to the early Welsh meter, *cywydd*, first made popular in the fourteenth century. Both poets celebrate their Welsh ancestry in their work, and another

---

[9] Personal email with the author, September 6, 2016.

interesting parallel between Morgan and Rash is that in the most influential essays written on each poet, and the ones that essentially served as their introductions to a general poetry-reading audience, commentators on their work mention the early Welsh alliterative method called *cynghanedd*.[10] The sound effect is similar to the Old English poetics found in *Beowulf*, though the repetitions are less ordered, and can offer greater surprise for the reader and flexibility for the poet. Rash's poem "The Corpse Bird" illustrates the chiming and echoing of sounds and demonstrates the seven-syllable verse line.

> Bed-sick she heard the bird's call
> fall soft as a pall that night
> quilts tightened around her throat,
> her gray eyes narrowed, their light
> gone as she saw what she'd heard
> waiting for her in the tree
> cut down at daybreak by kin
> to make the coffin, bury
> that perch around her so death
> might find one less place to rest.

The poem's opening line is a feast of sound chimes. Dividing the line into two measures, "Bed-sick she heard / the bird's call," one hears the echo of "b" in *bed* and *bird's*, the "s" of *sick* and *she* picked up by *bird's*, and then, in a perfect turn, a vowel chime with the internal rhyme of *heard* and *bird's*. Anthony Hecht wrote a glowing introduction to Rash's second poetry collection *Among the Believers*, and he paid special attention to "The Corpse Bird":

> What moves and impresses in these lines is related to a dramatic use of enjambment, to the poet's ability to force us beyond a point at which we had expected to rest in accepted resolution, and deliberately to confound a cluster of events; the fact of her "seeing" what she has heard as the light departs from her eyes (emphasized by the

---

[10] See Anthony Hecht's introduction for *Among the Believers* and William Harmon's 1981 essay "Robert Morgan's Pelagian Georgics," published in *Parnassas*.

ambiguity of "narrowed," which can be read as either a verb or an adjective).... The lines, the small events, blend and flow together in a seamless utterance that is full of mystery and drama.[11]

Many of the characteristics Hecht examines as the power of such concise and intricate poems emerge even more fully in Rash's third collection of poems, *Raising the Dead*. Two consecutive poems in this volume display Rash at his most masterful and deeply felt. "Watuaga County, 1803" chronicles the drowning of a mountain family in a flood and begins with these powerful lines:

> Night falling, river rising
> into the cabin, a hound
> howling on the porch, and then
> an unbuckling from bank roots.

The drama of the scene, wherein the cabin (which the speaker calls "covenant of that failed ark") slips into the flood waters, surges on the sudden and tragic nature of the event described but also on the insistence of Rash's meter and on his rolling effect of catching the long "i" sound in the opening line and the "b" sound in the fourth line. "In Dismal Gorge," the poem that follows "Watuaga County, 1803" in *Raising the Dead*, has a similarly tragic theme as well as a similarly effective poetic design.

> The lost can stay lost down here,
> in laurel slicks, false-pathed caves.
> Too much too soon disappears.
>
> On creek banks clearings appear,
> once homesteads. Nothing remains.
> The lost can stay lost down here,
>
> like Tom Clark's child, our worst fears
> confirmed as we searched in vain.
> Too much too soon disappears.

---

[11] Anthony Hecht, introduction to Ron Rash, *Among the Believers*, xii.

How often this is made clear
where cliff shadows pall our days.
The lost can stay lost down here,

stones scattered like a river
in drought, now twice-buried graves.
Too much too soon disappears,

lives slip away like water.
We fill our Bibles with names.
The lost can stay lost down here.
Too much too soon disappears.

The repetition of designated lines presents an apparent difficulty, but
Rash imposes the additional challenge of rhyme scheme, which is generally not a requirement of the villanelle. Rash employs the poetic tools of a
master builder, including slant rhyme and alliteration, and maintains his
signature seven-syllable line. The forms are often invisible, or nearly so, in
the poems of both Ron Rash and Robert Morgan, hidden by design because both poets understand that craft without substance is merely exercise, and skill on overt display diminishes the achievement.

One of Ron Rash's finest poems is "Three A.M. and the Stars Were
Out,"[12] from his 2011 collection, *Waking*. The poem recounts, in first person, the story of an aged veterinarian making a middle-of-the-night house
call to a remote farm. Most of the action of the poem takes places inside
the speaker's mind as he makes the long drive to the farm, where he knows
"what's to be done best done with / rifle or shotgun" (lines 38–39). We are
given access to his memories and speculations as well as to his doubts and
anxieties. It is also perhaps the most masterful display of technical facility,
and of driving that facility to serve and enlarge the effect of a piece of
writing, in all of Rash's work. Beyond the remarkable control of voice and
tone, Rash's command of syntax and sentence structure distinguish this
poem. The most startling formal detail is that the first sixty-four lines are
one single sentence. This dramatic technique creates a propulsive, ram-

---

[12] Rash also published a prose version of this scenario, with the same title, as
a short story in his 2013 collection, *Nothing Gold Can Stay*.

bling sensation about what the speaker reveals of his many years of experiences traveling country backroads. That long, musing, associative opening is followed by a one-line sentence: "Though sometimes it all works out" (line 65). The startling juxtaposition of those two sentences is eye-opening and generates a heightened sense of gravity around the one-line sentence.

"Three A.M. and the Stars Were Out" reads like a Shakespearean soliloquy, except there is no reason to assume that the words in the car have been spoken aloud. No specific implied listener to what the speaker has to say is identified, so the piece is not quite a dramatic monologue (though the tone and situation could easily be imagined in a Robert Browning poem) but more of an interior monologue, in which the thoughts of the speaker are uninterrupted by a narrator. This is a form of stream-of-consciousness writing, a once-experimental Modernist technique that now feels as familiar as third-person omniscient narration, because all readers understand the design and the purpose of entering into the stream of a character's thoughts. Readers understand what is being revealed and why it has taken a form: the thought process itself made visible, generally associated with the way characters think out loud in plays.

Rash addresses poetic form, and literary inheritance, most directly in "Dylan Thomas," also from his collection *Waking*:

> Scawmy, gray-souled November
> blinds the whale-road, pall draper
> over this ship bearing one
> whose name means *of the ocean*
> in a language he denied
> allegiance to, though his lines
> rang with *cynghanedd*—English
> reined in by Celtic music,
> stitched tight as the coracle
> that wombed Taliesin—tribal
> rain-downs of sounds, not enough:
> a small people lose their tongue
> one poet at a time. Talent-
> squanderer, fraud, miscreant,
> apt sobriquets for a life
> lived badly between the lines.

The coast recedes. Last gulls cry.
Down in the hold his drunk wife
smokes and flirts with the seamen
who play cards on his coffin.

Rash rebukes Thomas for abandoning, even denying, the language of his people, even though the key characteristics of the language do not leave him. Rash finds a way to acknowledge poetic tradition and to recognize how it emanates from poetry even when it has been openly rejected. Through his own destructive choices, Thomas has wasted his opportunity to be the great poet of the Welsh tongue, and the final humiliation is that his poorly chosen wife does not even mourn him after his death. Interestingly, Robert Morgan also has a recent poem that redresses Dylan Thomas and his most famous poem, "Do Not Go Gentle into That Good Night." In his response poem "Go Gentle," from *Terroir*, Morgan asserts that Thomas does not really understand the feelings that surround the end of a parent's life, and that no one would truly want to see a loved one struggle against an easeful death.

Rash varies his formal approaches throughout his work, as does Morgan, but the use of the seven-syllable pattern persists from his earliest poems through his most recent. In the opening lines to "Wet Moon," in the New Poems section of Rash's *Poems: New and Selected*, the pattern moves fluidly through lyric reflection as well as spoken dialogue:

"Come look," my grandmother said,
"the moon's shed its skin, see how
big and bright," and when I asked
where the old skin was she laughed,
sent me to bed, where I waked,
looked out the window and found
moonglow draped on the barn roof
for a tall ladder to lean
against the wood slats and raise
a finger, brush the cool skin
that had once been cloaked with stars.

This is not the first instance of Rash using formal devices to give shape and rhythm to spoken language; in fact, he has used this technique in his novels. In *Serena* (2008), many lines of dialogue are written out in iambic pentameter. In his 2015 novel, *Above the Waterfall*, he experiments with Gerard Manley Hopkins's method of "sprung rhythm," in which his character, Becky Shytle, begins to emulate Hopkins in her speech and even in the way she thinks to herself. Because poetry is an ancient mode of expression, and because its origins lie in the oral tradition of songs and stories, dialogue and poetic forms come together in a natural bond.

In a technological society, ways of doing things change rapidly—new means replace old means—but in Appalachia, entire ways of life have changed in three generations. This is not to say that Appalachia was ever a non-technological society, but simply that in this region the means and the ends of survival were often indistinguishable, that a life on the land is synchronous with a livelihood drawn from the land. In urban settings, people commute to work rather than walk, they cook on a gas or electric stove rather than coal, they work on a laptop rather than a typewriter; in these instances, the means change, but ends remain the same. As the economy of operating a small farm becomes unviable, both the means and the ends of the lives it has supported must change. Robert Morgan and Ron Rash represent a generation of Appalachian writers who witnessed firsthand, mostly in the lives of their parents, the shift away from a primarily agricultural livelihood. These poets record not only the work and ways of living but also the change itself, and its attendant losses. One could call their work commemorative, and as memory is mother of the muses, that would be an accurate claim, but in another sense, these writers, and so many others in the region, give history a second life. Robert Morgan and Ron Rash take Eliot's claim about "the historical sense"[13] seriously, and by embracing certain aspects of poetry's long tradition, such as syllabic verse forms, they invoke the past as a deeper layer, a substrata, of life in the continuously evolving present moment.

Works Cited

Eliot, T. S. *Selected Prose*. New York: Harcourt and FSG, 1975. Print.

---

[13] In his seminal essay, "Tradition and the Individual Talent," T. S. Eliot declares the necessity of a poet developing what he calls "the historical sense" if he is to mature as an artist.

Harmon, William. "Robert Morgan's Pelagian Georgics." *Parnassus: Poetry in Review* 9, no. 2 (1981): 5–30.

Hecht, Anthony. "Introduction." *Among the Believers*, by Ron Rash. Oak Ridge, TN: Iris Press, 2000. xi–xv.

Hoagland, Tony. "Fear of Narrative and the Skittery Poem of Our Moment." *Poetry*. March 2006.

Morgan, Robert. *At the Edge of the Orchard Country.* Middletown, CT: Wesleyan University Press, 1987.

———. *Good Measure.* Baton Rouge: LSU Press, 1993.

———. *Sigodlin.* Middletown, CT: Wesleyan University Press, 1990.

———. *Topsoil Road.* Baton Rouge: LSU Press, 2000.

Rash, Ron. *Among the Believers.* Oak Ridge, TN: Iris Press, 2000.

———. *Poems: New and Selected.* New York: Ecco HarperCollins, 2016.

———. *Raising the Dead.* Oak Ridge, TN: Iris Press, 2002.

———. *Waking.* Spartanburg: Hub City Press, 2011.

Wright, Charles. *Halflife.* Ann Arbor: University of Michigan Press, 1988.

5

The Return of the Native Speaker:
Maurice Manning's Dramatic Voices[1]

Let me begin by admitting that I scrapped most of my original title, which included the phrase "Appalachian Dramatic Monologues," largely because the paper did not turn out to be what I thought it was going to be—I blame this entirely on Maurice Manning, whose poems almost never go where one expects them to go. In fact, one of the joys of reading these poems is recognizing how often they surprise and how seldom they go down the well-trodden paths. In his poem "Merlin," Ralph Waldo Emerson has his angels say that we "mount to paradise / By the stairway of surprise," and reading Manning's work reminds us that poets will always find new ways to express the mysteries and experiences of our lives. So I have changed my title because most of the terms I first thought I would use ended up feeling too limiting once I tried to apply them to individual examples of Manning's poems. "Appalachian" seemed to narrow the scope of the poems to an actual geographic setting they did not specify, and "dramatic monologue" didn't quite cover the entire range of voices and perspectives in the poems I wanted to discuss. One thing I kept from the original title is my allusion to my favorite Thomas Hardy novel, *The Return of the Native*. The novel tells the story of a man who returns from a cosmopolitan life in Paris to his homeland, Egdon Heath, a provincial

---

[1] Presented at Emory & Henry College Literary Festival, October 25, 2012.

English village, and must readjust his life to its former circumstances. The reference suggests a fresh engagement with old ways and also allows me the phrase "native speaker," which I want to use to designate the voice we hear in Maurice Manning's poems.

Manning makes very old techniques feel brand new, and I believe this is one of the signatures of his poetry. Poets have always used dramatic techniques, such as having several voices speak in their poems, but they haven't always turned them over to the kinds of characters to whom Manning entrusts his poems: the rural, the uneducated, and wild, imaginative, even eccentric children. What I continuously find in Manning's poems is sympathy, a kind and yet never condescending feeling toward the humble, the remote, and the common. In a range of voices—sometimes bawdy, sometimes elegiac, and ranging widely between the two—we encounter the materials of real lives as well as the fabrics of mythic adventures. Maurice Manning gives voice, a living speaking voice, to experiences and especially to people that haven't been heard from very much before.

I will say a little about what I mean by "dramatic voices," or dramatic poems. The textbook definition of this is "A poem that reveals 'a soul in action' through the speech of one character in a dramatic situation. The character is speaking to an identifiable but silent listener at a dramatic moment in the speaker's life."[2] For my purposes, I'd like to contrast that with what I'll call lyric poems, or poems of "personal feeling." Some of the best-known poems are in this lyric voice: "My mistress' eyes are nothing like the sun"; "When I have fears that I may cease to be"; "I wandered lonely as a cloud"; "I celebrate myself, and sing myself, / and what I assume you shall assume"; "Because I could not stop for death, / he kindly stopped for me"; and finally, and more recently, "I saw the best minds of my generation destroyed by madness, starving hysterical naked." I choose these examples not only because they are famous but also to show the range of kinds, or styles, of poetry they represent, from Shakespeare to the Beat Poets, and all the best in between—Keats and Wordsworth, Whitman and Dickinson. Also, you could trace this back to the ancient Greek lyrics, and the fragments we have from Sappho would fit nicely into the same category of voice. I think we could safely call this the dominant mode of literary poetry: the *lyric*, or the *personal lyric*, or the poem of *personal feeling*. In poems

---

[2] William Harmon and Hugh Holman, "Dramatic Monologue," in *A Handbook to Literature* (Upper Saddle River, NJ: Prentice Hall, 2003), 164.

that veer from this mode and put the voice of the poem in the hands (or mouths, really) of a speaker definitively not the poet, we have a significant variation and, presumably, a significant goal for the outcome.

"Dramatic monologue" is a fairly technical term, referring to just one kind of "spoken" poem, and while the entirety of Manning's third book *Bucolics* fits comfortably into this category, much of his other work does not. However, I wanted to talk about more of his poems that are technically "dramatic monologues" and of what binds them all together, which is voice. None of the poems in *A Companion for Owls*, Manning's second book, and only a few of the poems in *Lawrence Booth's Book of Visions* fit into this category, yet all the poems in both collections do rely on what I think is the most important thread through all Manning's work so far, which is not only how the poems are spoken but also who speaks them.

For an example of the range of voices in Manning's work, let's consider the poem "A Dream of Ash and Soot," from near the end of his first collection, *Lawrence Booth's Book of Visions*. In this poem we hear the final chapter of the tense story of Booth's Mad Daddy, who is also called Ole Dreadful Daddy, Ole Black Jack Daddy, Crackshot Daddy, Bad Gamble Daddy, and many other versions of that in different poems. Here we also see how Manning contrasts one voice, that of young Lawrence, with the wild pronouncements of Mad Daddy.

Most significant poets have what we would call a recognizable voice—any regular reader of contemporary poetry would be able to look at three poems on a table and tell us which was written by John Ashbery, which by Mary Oliver, and which by Billy Collins. Now, there are at least fifty living poets whom I could have listed above, but the three I chose are deliberate: in each case, the Voice that is the poet's signature has become so reliable that it has become a weakness (one might have said predictable, repetitive, and self-imitating, but one is generally more polite than that).

In his book *The Situation of Poetry*, Robert Pinsky observes the following: "The use of a borrowed voice of alter-identity, as speaker or central character partly distinct from the poet, constitutes one of the most widely noted...and fundamental aspects of modernism."[3] He also notes that "such poetry uses the dramatic mode as a way to keep intact a kind of silence or

---

[3] Robert Pinsky, *The Situation of Poetry* (Princeton and Oxford: Princeton University Press, 1976), 14.

ambivalence."[4] Pinsky goes on to discuss poems by T. S. Eliot and Robert Lowell, and their continuation of the ironic modes of Robert Browning and Alfred, Lord Tennyson. To me, this demonstrates the difference between giving and taking. What Manning does in *Bucolics* is to *give* the fieldhand a voice and an audience, which he has not historically had; whereas Tennyson takes, or "borrows," the voice of Ulysses, a well-defined and powerful presence in Western literature since its inception. Tennyson uses that voice in an unexpected way—he shows a surprising dissatisfaction in the role Ulysses plays after he has made his long journey home. Manning's fieldhand is just the opposite. By the end of *Bucolics*, the fieldhand is very content with his humble lot in life.

T. S. Eliot wrote a good deal on poetry as drama and on dramatic poetry, and in one instance he writes "A Dialogue on Dramatic Poetry," in which one speaker asks, "What great poetry is not dramatic? Who is more dramatic than Homer or Dante?"[5] This may be a good time to remember that Eliot originally intended for the title of his colossal poem, *The Waste Land*, to be *He Do the Police in Different Voices*. This was before Ezra Pound had his say in editing the poem, and fortunately we ended up with *The Waste Land* instead. However, I don't hear much Eliot, or much Modernist influence at all, in Manning's work, unless you count Robert Frost, who, like Thomas Hardy and Rainer Maria Rilke, is more of a bridge from the nineteenth century into the early twentieth than a "High Modernist."

As we heard earlier, in *Lawrence Booth's Book of Visions* Manning employs a whole cast of characters, much like in a play, to tell the poems mostly in third person. In the following book, *A Companion for Owls*, subtitled *Being the Commonplace Book of D. Boone, Long Hunter, Back Woodsman, &c.*, the poems are all in the voice of Daniel Boone, with a surprising sophistication and eloquence from Boone despite his lack of formal learning. The medium, though, is not the spoken voice of Boone but rather his written, composed voice: a commonplace book is not necessarily addressed to any pubic audience but more to the private self, for the purpose of personal memory and record-keeping. The most important quality this "giv-

---

[4] Ibid.

[5] T. S. Eliot, "A Dialogue on Dramatic Poetry" (1928), in *Selected Essays, 1917–1932* (New York: Harcourt: 1932), 31.

ing voice" to disparate speakers displays is sympathy, and readers are offered an unguarded insight into the lives of Booth, Boone, and the fieldhand in *Bucolics*, Manning's third volume. *Bucolics* is the crown jewel of the
first three books, and I think this poem, number V, will show why:

V

You're the hay maker Boss
You light the candle in the sun
Dip the water in the rain
O for the whole big picture
You're the painter Boss I know
It's you the biggest boss of all
You must have a sack full of wind
Somewhere a barrel full of salt
A recipe for stone things like that
You keep them close to your chest
You keep your secrets Boss
You flash a yellow eye then crow
Away like you're a rooster Boss
Sometimes you're like a fox[6]

In this poem, we get a sense of the relationship between the speaker,
our unnamed fieldhand that I mentioned earlier, and the "Boss," his nick-
name for God. The fieldhand speaks to "Boss" in a familiar, even playful,
manner, yet by the end of the poem, one sees the wariness he maintains
toward his "Boss," who never reveals or shares anything about himself. All
the poems in *Bucolics* are titled only by Roman numerals, and none are
punctuated. All are spoken by the fieldhand, who addresses all his
thoughts and musings, and most interestingly his questions, directly to the
"Boss," who, as one might expect, never speaks back. *Bucolics* marks the
most definite example of the dramatic monologue in Manning's body of
work, and it fits the textbook definition I mentioned earlier, with a single
speaker distinct from the author, and an identified but silent listener.

In all the reviews I found for *Bucolics*, not one mentioned the poet
George Herbert, which I find curious, because more than half of Herbert's

---

[6] Maurice Manning, "V," in *Bucolics* (Orlando: Harcourt, 2007), 7.

poems are direct addresses to God. I find that an interesting precursor; and given that Herbert lived from 1593 until 1633, making him a younger contemporary of Shakespeare and Marlowe, he fits nicely into my premise that Maurice Manning has given us an approach to poetry that feels very new and fresh by reinventing, or reinvigorating, approaches and techniques that are very old. Herbert is generally considered one of the metaphysical poets, about whom Helen Gardner wrote the following: "Their style was characterized by wit and metaphysical conceits—far-fetched or unusual similes or metaphors, such as in Andrew Marvell's comparison of the soul with a drop of dew."[7]

Consider these lines from Herbert's "The Pilgrimage" as a companion piece to some of the sentiments from Manning's *Bucolics*:

> At length I got unto the gladsome hill,
>   Where lay my hope,
>   Where lay my heart; and climbing still,
>   When I had gain'd the brow and top,
> A lake of brackish waters on the ground
>   Was all I found.
>
> With that abash'd and struck with many a sting
>   Of swarming fears,
>   I fell, and cry'd, Alas my King!
>   Can both the way and end be tears?[8]

This passage from Herbert expresses much of the same doubt and worry that Manning's fieldhand shows in the early poems from *Bucolics*. Even the setting is the same, with the speaker asking his question from a pastoral landscape. A bucolic poem is a rural, pastoral poem, specifically about the lives of shepherds. The word comes from the Greek "Bukalos," which translates as "neatherd," or cattle herder (rather than sheep herder, maybe a small distinction to us now, but those would have been very different jobs). Even in the ancient literature, there are more poems about

---

[7] Helen Gardner, *The Metaphysical Poets* (Oxford UP, London, 1957), 3.

[8] George Herbert, "The Pilgrimage," in *Poems* (New York: Everyman's Library, 2004), 77–78.

rustic life than there are poems told in the voices of rustics, seemingly always a way of life both oversimplified and underrepresented.

As I was starting to begin articulating my thoughts on what happens in Maurice Manning's poetry, a happy coincidence occurred: I received a book in the mail that I had been looking forward to for some time. In honor of the scholar M. H. Abrams's one hundredth birthday, Norton published a collection of his most recent essays, titled *The Fourth Dimension of a Poem*. Abrams is best known for writing one of the greatest books of literary criticism ever published, *The Mirror and the Lamp*, published in 1953 (and *Natural Supernaturalism* from 1973 is almost as important). I have a personal relation to Abrams that goes back to my graduate student days at Cornell, when Abrams—he was only about ninety years old then— still roamed the hallways of Goldwin Smith.

For Abrams, the first three dimensions of the reading of a poem are fairly straightforward: one, the visible cues and signals that alert us that we are to read the text as poetry and not prose; two, the sound of the words as they are read aloud or imagined by the reader; and three, the most important aspect, the meaning of the words we read or hear. The fourth dimension is more elusive, "mysterious," he calls it, which is the "enunciating of the great variety of speech-sounds that constitute the words of the poem."[9] Abrams considers this the "material body" of the poem, given by our physical speaking of or imagining the spoken words. This reminded me of what Manning says in his essay "Dark Matter," about how speech floats around in the air, the vast majority of it never recorded, and alive only in its moment of utterance; Manning's dramatic poems, attending to the Fourth Dimension of Poetry, give body to disembodied speech, to language we would never hear unless he caught it and made it materialize on the page and eventually in our throats and voices.

My initial title included the word "Appalachian," and that was partly to indicate what I felt was a geographic designation—the setting of the poems. I decided that was debatable, or at least not definitive in the texts themselves, so I removed it. However, the term "Appalachian" also bears associations with a particular literary history and lineage, one in which Manning's work rests very comfortably, and this is why I bring it up again. Manning follows a generation of poets from the region—and who write

---

[9] M. H. Abrams, "The Fourth Dimension of a Poem," in *The Fourth Dimension of a Poem and Other Essays* (New York: Norton, 2012), 2.

extensively about the region—that produced an unprecedented fruitfulness in both quality and national recognition. Charles Wright may be the most widely known of this group (plus he's from Tennessee, and well...what can I say?), but I wouldn't consider him part of the core group who make up the poetry contingent of what is sometimes called the Appalachian Renaissance: those would be Fred Chappell, Jeff Daniel Marion, Jim Wayne Miller, and Robert Morgan. The poems of Maurice Manning share many qualities with these predecessors, including the careful observation of rural landscapes, the mysteries, fears, and wonders of childhood, and the sounds of local speech. Manning shares with these poets an attention to what Robert Morgan has called *terroir*, the particular qualities of a place and how those qualities infuse what grows there.

Where Maurice Manning differs from that earlier generation of Appalachian poets lies in how he uses regional speech. I feel there is something afoot recently with Manning, and also Frank X. Walker, among others, giving the voice of their poems over entirely to what I'm calling native speakers, rather than having a more traditional lyric speaker represent dialect through memory or quotation of another character, such as an older relative. For a brief example, I would suggest how Fred Chappell (the preceding poet most similar in style and content to Manning) integrates the voices of other speakers in "My Grandmother Washes Her Vessels" and "My Grandmother Washes Her Feet." I do not want to suggest that those earlier poets never used dramatic speakers—Jim Wayne Miller's "The Brier Sermon" and Jeff Daniel Marion's *The Chinese Poet Awakens* collection are interesting examples of that technique—but only that none of those poets use it as extensively as Manning and that his usage places Manning in a long tradition of Southern and Appalachian poets, though one that is largely distinct from his most obvious and recent predecessors.

I would like to consider one more poem in some detail, this time with a long excerpt from the title piece of Manning's most recent collection:

The Common Man

Well, it's me, this time; I'm sitting here
In a farmhouse. Things have happened here,

Besides the sun and chimney smoke,
But most of the time it's pretty quiet.

In the cemetery down the lane
There's a stone for a long-gone woman named

America, wife of so-and-so;
Another woman's maiden name

Was Silvertooth. Both women died
Two hundred years ago. The lane

Ran through the stream back then and I've found
One half of a rust bit to prove it.

I suppose I'm common enough. I come
From this dirt, from dark Kentucky ground

Steeped in blood and steep beneath
My feet. All my life, it's always up

And down. I know the lay of the land,
And like any rude provincial man,

I am content with what I know.

Here we have the opening movement of a beautiful poem about local history; about the wonder of words, including proper names; and especially about identity, announced at the opening and defined at the end of this segment. But whose identity is it? Is it Maurice Manning's? Well, that's hard to say, and in the end it's not terribly important. This excerpt shows the difficulty in drawing with permanent marker the lines between dramatic poems and poems of personal feeling.

A wonderful interview with Manning just appeared in the current, "live," issue of *Still: The Journal*, conducted presumably (though anonymously) by Marianne Worthington in late September 2012. So it's brand new, the latest statement on our topic, and I'll quote a passage that sheds valuable light on this issue of voice and speaker in poems. After a question about dramatic poetry, Manning responds with the following:

MM: So much of *Lawrence Booth* is autobiographical material that I felt embarrassed writing about it in first person. And then, *A Companion for Owls* was in first person but in the imagined voice of a historical figure. And then, *Bucolics*, well, at one point when I was working on that book, I thought, "now this is *my* voice." But now that I look back on it, I think, "well, no, that's not so much my voice after all." Then when I was working on *The Common Man* I thought, "OK, now, *this* is my voice."

Still: Does that mean that you are still searching for your voice?

MM: I don't know. I know that's been one of the larger processes of writing for me. I think fiction writers are off this hook on "finding your voice." Nobody questions Herman Melville writing in the voice of a character named Ishmael. In novels written in first person, in the voice of a character, nobody says to the novelist, "is this your voice?" It's just understood that fiction requires the writer to imagine voices other than his or her own. Writing in different voices is an issue for me as a poet. Am I writing in what feels like wholly my own voice? I would say I have moved toward that. And I'm glad to have moved toward that. But I also think that if you're writing in your "own" voice, you tend to write with a great deal of seriousness and earnestness and gravity. If you're not feeling obliged to be wholly yourself on the page, for me, it's allowed a greater range of imagination and some humor and more variety. I've enjoyed that, and I think that the poems I'm writing now do feel much more like the voice in my mind.[10]

Maybe we can take that as a preview of the poems ahead.[11]

I want to come back to final section of the poem "The Common Man"—since we left our speaker he has eaten a turnip, "as raw as love"; his dog ran in circles; he watched the moon come up. And this is a page and half later. Nothing much is happening here, right? Well, on the surface it might seem that way, but let's pick up there and hear the poem until the

---

[10] Manning, interview by Marianne Worthington, *Still: The Journal*, September 2012.

[11] I would encourage you to go online and read the rest of this interview—it's all wonderful and insightful, plus it ends with an awesome picture of Maurice's farm dogs, which makes me want to get about three more. See www.stilljournal.net/interview-maurice.php.

end:

...And that's
The way things are, a story here

And there, but mostly here. There's hope
In a world that's slowly happening,

According to its own design,
If you want to call it that. Oh, yes,

There's sorrow here, not a day goes by
That isn't stabbed with common sorrow,

With death, regret, and loneliness,
And some of us get a bigger portion

Of the little tragedies. That's not
Uncommon, though, now is it?

I've had my share and I'll have more,
And so will you. What matters most

Is not so much what happened once,
But what will happen next. Who knows?

And then the moon rose up behind
The barn and I went out to see it.

And then I went to sleep, and then
I dreamed, and in my dream I saw

A red light tumble like a leaf
Through the sky; in the morning something else

Was going to happen, I knew it, but
I knew I didn't know it yet.

The great twentieth century Polish poet Czeslaw Milosz claimed that when we write a poem about a moment, or an object, we hold it up to the light, we take it out of the flow of ordinary time or objects, and we "valorize" it. I love that idea—we hear "value" and "validate" and also get the idea that we give it courage, strength to move ahead, and that to me is what "The Common Man" does for a life that claims to be nothing special.

Thanks for your thoughtful attention, and thanks to Maurice Manning for these poems that continue to illuminate the voices we might not otherwise hear. I am not alone in looking forward to his next book of poems, titled, as I have read, *The Gone and the Going Away* and due out in spring 2013. I am of the opinion that Manning's poems have gotten richer and more exciting, and are also reaching deeper levels of sympathy and experience, with each successive volume. Most poets would have had to stop with *Bucolics*, because it's hard to imagine topping it—I am sure there will be readers in one hundred years who look back on our time and say that it is the best book of American poetry of the first decade of the 2000s—but I contend that Manning did top it with *The Common Man*, and I hope that my discussion of the title poem shows a bit of why. We are reading a poet who reproduces the beauty and nuance of the country landscape, who reinvigorates the soundscapes of our poetry, who tells one hilarious tale, I kid you not (as one of Manning's speakers likes to say), and, most importantly as I see it, who gives us not just one voice but a whole casts of voices that help us appreciate and savor such treasures as the world has to offer.

6

Celebrating the Wide Embrace of
Jeff Daniel Marion[1]

I knew the name, the reputation, and the poetry of Jeff Daniel Marion long before I had the occasion to meet the man himself. As an undergraduate at The University of Tennessee in Knoxville during the mid-1990s, I was immersed in a vibrant literary community on campus, with inspiring poetry teachers like Connie Jordan Green, Marilyn Kallet, and Arthur Smith, and classmates like Heather Dobbins, Charlotte Pence, Melissa Range, Daniel Roop, and Jennifer Vasil, who were not only wonderful poets but also great friends. I attended readings by legendary poets such as Galway Kinnell and Linda Gregg. However, Knoxville's literary life didn't end at the edge of campus, and a name that came up again and again in bookstore circles and the local papers was Jeff Daniel Marion. I had no idea yet that the same widely regarded poet I was hearing about would someday become one of my closest and most treasured friends and mentors, Danny Marion.

I spent many afternoons during those days in bookstores, searching the shelves for names I had heard in literature classes and looking for interesting titles that could become my own discoveries. My favorite used bookstore was a hideaway in the back of Jackson Avenue Antique Mall in

---

[1] Presented at Carson-Newman University, April 12, 2013.

Knoxville's Old City, which later became the Book Eddy and is now Central Avenue Books. I would browse for hours, self-educating, as Ted Kooser says all poets must do. I recall opening one nicely bound paperback with a striking hourglass image on the cover and finding on the inside flap, in the most distinct handwriting, the signature "Jeff Daniel Marion, 1969." Of course, this date was almost a decade before Marion's first poetry collection, *Out in the Country, Back Home*, was published. The book was Alfred Kazin's essay collection, *Contemporaries*, and though I had no idea who Alfred Kazin was, I knew that if Jeff Daniel Marion, about whom I had heard so much, had read this book once, then I needed to buy this book and do the same. Upon closer inspection, I was delighted to find an essay by Kazin, who was to become one of my guides through literary criticism, titled "Good-by to James Agee." James Agee had already become one of my local heroes, but I still find it a lovely happenstance that the signature of one of East Tennessee's greatest poets led me to a classic essay about one of East Tennessee's greatest prose writers.

My first face-to-face meeting with Jeff Daniel Marion came a couple of years later, while I was still an undergraduate at the University of Tennessee. Danny and his wife at that time, the poet Linda Parsons Marion, selected my poem "White Scars" as the first-place winner of the 1997 Libba Moore Gray Poetry Prize, given by the Knoxville Writers' Guild. I was invited to read my poem at a reception at the beautiful Laurel Theater in the Fort Sanders area of Knoxville, from the same stage where I had watched enthralled as Galway Kinnell read, recited, and half-sung his amazing poems. My parents and uncle drove in from Sharps Chapel for the reading, and many friends from school came, but the highlight of the evening for me was my first conversation with Danny Marion. I was surprised by how seriously he took me, a fairly scrappy-looking undergraduate who had somehow managed to beat out some real writers for a poetry prize. I was struck by how intently he listened to what I had to say and by how many questions he asked me. He seemed impressed that I admired James Wright's poetry and that I had read Cormac McCarthy and Wilma Dykeman. Danny asked what I planned to do after my time at UT, and I somewhat bashfully said that I was thinking about applying to graduate schools, maybe even to pursue poetry writing. He smiled, made some encouraging comments about my poems, and offered to read more of my work. Then he inquired about what schools I was considering. "Have you thought about Cornell?" he asked. I think I laughed out loud and said,

"That's kind of a long shot, don't you think?" Then Danny said exactly what I needed to hear at that time: "Well, I don't know about that. You've got the talent to try for a long shot or two." After our conversation, Danny offered to write an informal letter on my behalf to his friend Robert Morgan, a professor at Cornell, and this undoubtedly helped open a door for me that I never would have imagined otherwise.

As I approach my fortieth birthday, I can look back over my life so far and pick a handful of days that set the course for what my future would become. That evening in the Laurel Theater when I met Danny Marion is one of those days, and not just because it led me to Cornell, where I would study with Robert Morgan and A. R. Ammons and linger in the presence of great minds like M. H. Abrams, Dan McCall, and so many others. That evening opened an ongoing conversation with Danny Marion that has lapsed only on a few occasions since, and hardly ever for more than a week or two at a time in the decade since I moved back to East Tennessee. From the beginning, this conversation involved poets we admired; movies that excited us; restaurants we would have to be out of our minds to miss; writers who should be better known; eccentric family members; and always new poems we were writing.

Marion's poetry takes its place now as one of the true jewels of Tennessee literature, on the high shelf alongside the works of James Agee, Cormac McCarthy, Peter Taylor, and Randall Jarrell. Though he was never my classroom teacher, I have learned as much from Danny Marion as from anyone about how to write an authentic, truthful, searching poem. I have learned from his example and from his line-by-line consideration of my poems. Many of the poems in my first book, *Tennessee Landscape with Blighted Pine*, are stronger because of his suggestions. Perhaps even the title of the book would have been different without his assurance that an unorthodox title could still be the book's true name. I needed confidence to let the book embrace the place that inspired so much of it.

One of the most persistent themes in the poetry of Jeff Daniel Marion is a recognition of transience, that what is here now can quickly vanish into the air. Water is a constant image in Marion's work, particularly his beloved Holston River, which is among the handful of muses for his poetry. Water and time are always moving, despite the occasional appearance of stillness or tranquility. I have learned through Marion's poems that there is not only uncertainty but also beauty in that state of motion. Many poems by Appalachian writers depict speakers searching for the lost past, a history they know about from elders and from community stories, but one that seems just on the cusp of fading away forever. Jeff Daniel Marion's work presents many examples of this search, most clearly in his poem "Ebbing & Flowing Spring." The poem opens with Marion's speaker returning to a familiar location, a springhouse, but finding it changed: the gourd used for dipping water has disappeared. Feeling the absence of the gourd, and the people who drank from it, the speaker traces a path back through time by recalling the stories told to him by an elderly woman named Matilda. Her stories cannot recreate the living past, but they can preserve its memory. The poem ends with the speaker accepting the pain of the icy water held in his cupped hands, "the cold / that aches and lingers,"[2] in exchange for the solace of drinking the fresh water, just as the pain of loss is exchanged for the consolation of memory.

Marion's poetry has been considered mostly in the context of Appalachian literature, and few writers have done more to establish and promote a sense of regional identity in their work. However, this identification risks offering a limited view of Marion's writing, which in fact engages with several national and global literary traditions. One of his most striking poetry collections is titled *The Chinese Poet Awakens*, in which the poems are spoken in the voice of a Chinese poet, probably an ancient observer, who is set down amongst the days and ways of East Tennessee. These are poems in the manner of Li Po, Han Shan, and Wang Wei, yet they "awaken" to the possibilities of life in the most unlikely of places. I had an alternate paper in mind for this festival, and it is a paper I still feel needs to be written, perhaps titled "Hosannas Forever: Jeff Daniel Marion and the American Transcendental Impulse." Marion's work is overdue to be considered as an accomplished representative of the central grain of American literary tradition, the grain that begins in Ralph Waldo Emerson and descends through Henry David Thoreau, Walt Whitman, and Emily Dickinson, out of the Flowering of the New England Mind, the American Renaissance, and into our contemporary literature.

Jeff Daniel Marion has just released his ninth collection of poems, *Letters to the Dead: A Memoir*, a book that illuminates the importance of what one learns from those who have passed before us and also how much one might still have to say to them. These poems are as much ode as elegy, and it is a testament to Marion's gifts that they are infused with as much

---

[2] Jeff Daniel Marion, "Ebbing & Flowing Spring."

joy as sadness. Marion's accomplishments are as impressive as they are various. He has performed distinguished work as an editor, letter-press publisher, and photographer. Marion has been awarded and recognized by countless organizations, including the 2011 James Still Award for Writing about the Appalachian South by the Fellowship of Southern Writers. To his friends, he is nearly as well regarded for his world-class collection of fountain pens, for his logbook of poems handwritten by their authors, for his expert palate for fine Indian cuisine, and for the shrine he has made to all things fine and literary at his house on the Holston River.

Through the years, my friendship with Danny Marion has grown beyond exchanging poems and trading opinions about overlooked writers, though we still do those things on a regular basis. We have grown into friends who talk about what it means to be a son, a husband, and a father; what it means to be a recorder of stories and lives, especially ones that might not get told or seen or understood if we fail to get them right in our telling. We talk about how to love places even after they have changed from what we originally loved; how to call places home even when their politics drive us half crazy and make us want to pull out the dwindling amounts of hair we have left between us. It seems that so many of our talks have become about how to love. About what home means. About how to be part of a place and how to show it to the rest of the world, if the world cares to look. These conversations have become acts of love, and they sustain me in every responsibility I maintain. The lesson Danny Marion's friendship has offered me is that no single role defines us, that we truly are large, multitudinous, and that the fullest life is the one taken in with the widest embrace.

7

On the Margins of the Writing World:
An Introduction to Karen Salyer McElmurray and Nancy Peacock's
Marginalia

Bethann Bowman and Jesse Graves[1]

BB: Jesse and I want to introduce you to Karen Salyer McElmurray's on-going work, the digital letters she publishes on the blog *Marginalia* with fellow writer Nancy Peacock. These writers exchange digital letters that explore how their daily struggles and joys fit into and sometimes threaten the balance of their writing lives. You might not know about Karen McElmurray's blog *Marginalia* even if you have read all her traditionally published work. The blog epistles she exchanges online with Nancy Peacock constitute a wonderful body of ongoing work.

In a post titled "A Little Departure…a virtual tour," McElmurray says about herself, "My most grounded self as a writer is from my home-

---

[1] Editor's Note: Bethann Bowman and Jesse Graves's presentation at the 2014 Emory & Henry College Literary Festival included Karen Salyer McElmurray's responses to direct questions. Speaking parts for Bowman, Graves, and McElmurray have been noted with BB, JG, or KM.

place. My blood, my voice, my hands, my heart are part and parcel of Eastern Kentucky, the mountains, Appalachia. The form my work takes comes from the place that made me. I hear those voices and translate them." She then describes her process and what to call her work: "I also sometimes think my work isn't 'a genre' at all. It's some fusion of poetry and lyric prose, with a big dash of Mark Rothko and Thomas Merton and Howard Finster in the mix." McElmurray also writes, "I love visionary work. I love work that has magic realist elements. I'm a fan of Toni Morrison, Leslie Marmon Silko. I'm also happiest when I'm reading about spirituality. Oh, and my garden. As my friend Mary Caroll-Hackett calls it, Dirt Church. The work of hands and earth." I just wanted to start with a section from the blog to give you an idea of how McElmurray self-identifies.

Careful, thoughtful, and brutally honest, the digital letters reveal much that is personal, and seemingly private, in a public forum. Like letters between all longtime correspondents, these develop connections and conversations across time. However, unlike most letters, they were never intended to be private. Throughout the letters, both writers discuss their attempts to create a space for Writing—capital W, Writing—in their lives and space for themselves. The blog accomplishes both while also eliminating the divide between private and public discourse.

In addition to eliminating this boundary, the blog form allows writers to incorporate live links. The live links take readers where you want them to go; it's convenient. And when we incorporate these live links and embed photographs, which there are some of as well, it's very cool. For example, McElmurray sometimes includes photographs to show where she is that week and the landscape surrounding her thoughts. The letters are between, for the most part, Nancy Peacock, a fellow writer, and Karen McElmurray. Sometimes there's a departure from that, which is partly because in this form everything is okay. The blog form can evolve, expand, contract, do nearly everything without losing its purpose. If I understand correctly, Karen's virtual tour blog post was created from a post she was tagged in on Facebook. Karen, is that right?

KM: It was an invitation, and each person who does it invites one more. I just did three.

BB: In this letter/blog post, she introduces us to other writers. She states, "Luisa tells me that when one is tagged, one must answer four basic questions about my work and creative process, and then tag (and briefly introduce) three or four writers who will then each continue to process

80

with their own writing friends." She tells us that she's working on a novel. Are you still on draft seven?

KM: Yeah.

BB: [speaking to the attendees] We know this detail about her because of the blog. We may not see the novel she is working on for another two years or longer, but we navigate through her blog post and find her draft. The links make this space an interactive space. It's a space where not only Nancy and Karen get to explore but where they allow us to explore too, to find writers we've never read, to think about things that we haven't thought about. Since Karen McElmurray suggests Sheldon Compton, I will likely pick up one of his works because I admire her work.

This interactive space is an expansion of what a letter is. Rather than just being correspondence with a single person, it becomes multidimensional as it draws in additional writers and readers. Some of the people she's recommending we might know—for example, Jane Hicks. I'm sure many of you know Jane Hicks. But do you know who Jane Hicks will recommend that you read? There's Jason Howard, but do you know who Jason Howard will recommend? That's just one of the things that can happen.

The blog becomes an exploration in a space for us as well. In the same way that we write in the margins of a book with an awareness of conversing with that text, we can interact with this ever-changing and growing blog form. Only now the margins are bigger and are no longer for individuals, but for communal consumption and investigation. They've created this space that is bigger and is not just between the text and the margin, but accessible to all of us. Blogs themselves were, at least originally, sort of on the margins of the writing world.

Yet, even though there is all this giving to us as an audience, the blog never ceases—the letters never cease—to be about self-exploration and intensely personal soul-searching. There is great sadness when McElmurray describes her visit with her dying mother, suffering end-stage Alzheimer's, but there is a revelation present too. There is horror and humor in Peacock and her husband trying desperately to clear a decaying squirrel along with last year's leaves out from under their gutter downspout. There are details and details and details of their lives. And a constant puzzling to figure out how to fit those into writing. And there's something much beyond that puzzling over detail. There is wisdom and reflection and a call to intimacy that the form of this public letter embodies.

I want to read from the September 2 letter [by McElmurray] about intimacy:

> To be intimate. Closely acquainted. Familiar. Informal. I know that as a writer I am not afraid of looking closely. You don't have to dig that deep, a friend told me once after she'd gone to a reading of mine. And yet I do. I do not want to be afraid of writing the body's flaws, the body's folds and reaches, the rough edges of its skin as I age, the musky gingko scent of sex. When I wrote the memoir about my son's birth and relinquishment to adoption, I wrote that moment where he left my body, the blood-scent. What else is there, but to be as true as I can, as real?

There is the intimacy exemplified in that blog entry. In offering the words, the spirit of the words, even the "blood-scent." Again. The writer has already sent these words into the world in her memoir, but memory brings them back here and asks us to hold them gently.

There are also writers listening here. To the space between the letters, to the comments people send in response to the blog, to the guest letter writers, and to the poets and writers of stories and hungry holy men who have come before. In a letter from April 13, 2014, McElmurray considers the words of Adrienne Rich: "We must use what we have to get what we desire." And that's what I think the blog is. So I'm going to ask Karen, if she will, to read—and I'll just leave her blog up—this passage, and you can stop wherever you like.

KM: This is a piece that I called "Care." And I think it was partly a response to Nancy writing me about, recently, the burden, the difficulty, the challenge, the blessing, all of it, of caring for her husband during a pretty serious illness right now. And so, this is one paragraph of my response. It's called "Care":

> Care. My life is a quilt made of the ways I have taken care. Take care out on them roads, my grandmother would say as I set out to drive the miles back to Virginia or Georgia, to Charlottesville or Lynchburg or Athens or Milledgeville, to all the places I've lived and worked. Care. Neat comments in the margins of my student's essays. Letters to them about observing and answering and questioning. Care. I teeter down a hallway toward the bathroom in some bar, careful not to slip and tumble after my fourth glass of wine. Care. Moving slowly toward love, being cautious, protective, giving

enough, but holding back, safe. Care. I used to need the house completely empty on a Saturday, so I could write. Had to have my then-
lover head to a coffee shop and stay there until I was finished for
the day. Care. I've learned, a former boss once told me, never to be
dependent on anyone. Care. No, I say, with more and more vehe-
mence these days. Or yes. This is what I want, what I do not want.
Care. How carefully do we tread the halls of academe, the pages of
the book, the moral compass of our lives? Care. I reach again and
again toward the heart, the deepest place, words that are not afraid
to say themselves. Fierce. Blunt. Politic. Real. Care. The face of a
lover, sleeping, how the eyes move in sleep. The friend who said
that having his first child was about "making the soul more fluid."
Care. Scatter seeds. Water lightly. Wait for sunlight.

JG: I'm really happy that Karen read that particular piece because it
was exactly the thing I wanted to lead with. I was struck by all the different
ways that care works its way through this blog, not just that one piece but
really throughout, as well as all the different ways in which this community
of writers, primarily Karen and Nancy, develop a weave of voices throughout. But you've got the two steady voices of Karen and Nancy to come
back to. Karen had me thinking about writing as a more solitary work and
how, like in the "Care" piece, if you're really working on something, you
kind of have to have a room of your own, probably the whole house, and
it'd be nice if the whole neighborhood was gone.

KM: Perhaps the world.

JG: Perhaps the world needs to just go away while you try and get
these lines right. And that really never happens. But the ways that writers
find to nurture each other and to take care of one another, I feel like there's
a lot of that going on throughout this blog. There's a lot of Nancy taking
care of something that Karen says, or Karen responding with a kind of
empathy or sympathy or generous feeling to something that Nancy has
said. And when we do an essentially solitary job, you have to find ways to
be with people and you have to find ways to make room for people. Another of my favorite entries is on this point. I sort of absorbed this blog
like reading a novel. Karen is right here, but she's also a character to me in
the story that I'm reading.

KM: This is so bizarre.

JG: It's a little weird for me too. Luckily, I had met Karen before, so
I could sort of figure out what she was supposed to be like, like we have to

do when we're reading a novel. I've not met Nancy, so Nancy really is kind of a character. I've read this blog in such a way that I can see the thing that they're working on; I can see the things that they are thinking about and how they are sharing those things with each other. One of my favorite entries is about Karen getting puppies and all the things that you have to sacrifice, like sleep and normal dreams. One of the things that Karen talks about is dreaming about some kind of massive squeegee to get up all the puppy pee. Getting up all through the night is like feeding a baby at times. And this was a funny entry mostly, but there was also a kind of serious question in that entry about the tradeoff. What else should I be doing with this time other than just caring for the puppy, playing with the puppy, all the things that this takes the place of? And to maybe think about all the ways in which the things that we love are set in opposition to each other. You know, there's tension between the thing that we love, to play with the puppy, and the work that we need to do. Nancy had a post about a student of hers who has a new baby and how to make time for that new baby and still be a writer. You will make time for the baby; it just insists that you will. But will you also make time to write something that day? Will you also make time to carve out whatever space you need in your head or in your surroundings to write?

Luisa, one of the guest bloggers, talks about that as well. She talks about remembering with an almost kind of physical sensation nursing her new baby with one arm and working on the lines of a poem with her other free hand. I thought, you know, I have done that myself, not the nursing part, but holding the baby and also writing or having a book open: these are two things, writing and teaching, writing and whatever your regular job is, writing and caring for the puppy, writing and trying to raise a small person up into the world. All these things are sometimes opposing each other.

Because for you students, you're writing papers and you're turning it in and then you're kind of done. You're done for a little while, but whoever you turn the papers in to, well, they take them home. And that's an ever-growing stack of paper that we are trying to find time to navigate. Sometimes you've got an idea for your own paper, you've got an idea for a poem, for a story, for whatever, and the thing that's between you and that idea is a stack of papers. These are two things that you care a lot about, and they are in opposition to one another. This blog is very clear-eyed about how you navigate those things that aren't necessarily working in unison: to do them would require the same space, the same time out of your life. How do you negotiate between them, being in such a solitary situation as writers often are? There's not that many people to talk about that sort of thing with. So many of the things came up in my own experience. I find that these writers, these very wise people, are also having these same experiences and talking about them and thinking about them, and sometimes coming to conclusions that I tend to incorporate; I tend to steal some of their conclusions from their own lives.

There is a real value to the kind of mentorship that happens between contemporaries. Here are two writers that are very far along in their accomplishments; they have both published significant bodies of work. It isn't like a beginner and an expert. Here are two people mentoring each other back and forth. I've been lucky enough to have some of those mentoring relationships with writers, with scholars, with people interested in my subject matter. Up to this point, it has mostly been older people, people who were my teachers, people who were writers I admired, who had sort of guided me along. These have been long-term friendships for me. There's such a value in finding a relationship, finding that dialogue with a mentor or with maybe someone who is your exact contemporary. Finding that person to share your thoughts and your fears and your hopes with.

If you're doing the thing that this person has made a career out of, you want to know how they've done that, you want to know how somebody has made writing poetry part of their life. Because certainly you don't get paid for writing poetry. I hope I'm not blowing up any career plans. Sometimes you get like ten dollars from a magazine. But you can't really make your living through poetry, so you have to have a regular job. For some of us, it's teaching; for some of us, it's a whole other thing. Wallace Stevens worked in advertising, and William Carlos Williams worked delivering babies. All those poets worked in various jobs that sort of make the money that allows you to write the poetry.

I want to say just a couple things about the pleasures of reading this blog. Because you are reading the words…you're reading a work that's being updated nearly every day.

KM: Nancy had written a draft that she was feeling very tentative about, and I think she was going to publish it.

JG: So you're really kind of reading this in the real time of somebody's life. There aren't many opportunities to do that in writing. The most recent contemporary novel that is published next week was written a few years ago. It's not the same ongoing thing as the blog. And the novelist has already moved on to the next one or two or three projects. So we're getting something that's really immediate. And there's something about reading the work in progress, reading the ideas that are being formulated, that I found really enjoyable. I found it really satisfying. And I feel a part of it.

KM: I'd just like to speak to that. There was a woman who kept a blog about her breast cancer journey. There's a series of photographs taken all during the last months of her life. I found that so incredibly moving. It was art taken so close to the bone. So that, what you're saying, it is real time. And I find that really fascinating.

JG: I do too. There's a real inventive quality to this blog to me. Even when we write…I don't know if any of you write letters to your friends; I don't know if you write letters to your parents; I doubt anybody does that anymore. You probably Facebook them or—

KM: Text.

JG: Or Tweet them. Whatever the format is. But even a letter takes some time to get there, and there is an immediacy to the blog that I really enjoyed. Also, I mentioned already about writing being the kind of work that you do by yourself, work that you do when you can get a quiet minute. I know these are composed that way, but there's a kind of collaboration in this project that I like a whole lot. It's not even just between two people. It's between two people and a community that they invite in and who make their own contribution, their own part of the collaboration. I like that so much; that has appealed to me for a long time.

Like I said, I mostly write poems and that's what I'm doing most afternoons; I'm working on them if I'm not teaching class. If I'm writing something, it's probably the draft of a poem. Though I also do other things; I also edit books of poems and collections of essays. I'm working on a couple of those things right now. That is where you get to have a collaborative opportunity if you are a writer. For the past year or so, I have been working with William Wright, a poet friend from Georgia, on this poem that has now grown into a book. He'll write a section and then I'll respond with a section, and then he'll write a section and then I'll respond with a section. It has been different from any other kind of work that I've ever done. Our voices are just different enough to create a kind of tension. I am always interested in how they are going to sound together, how they are going to work. We are not telling a story; we are not doing a narrative.

He is writing his poem and it stands alone; and I'm writing my piece and it stands alone. But they are sort of loosely working on a feeling or a topic or a subject.

This has been a great development for me, though I can't say for certain that these poems are any good. They seem pretty good to me right now because I don't have to show them to anybody. However, it's been a great development just to share that process with somebody, to share the working out of a kind of private experience with somebody else.

With my background in poetry, as well as a long study in lyric poetry as a genre, I see so much of lyricism in Karen's work. I see so many of the qualities that drew me into the language of poetry. I like to read novels; I like to read essays about poetry; and I like to read *Sports Illustrated* too. I just like to read, period. I like to read various analyses of last night's World Series game. I like to read; it's my thing, but lyric poetry is where I get off the bank into the stream. It's where I entered the conversation where one goes from being a reader to also being a writer. That has been my steadiest kind of reading, and I see so many qualities in Karen's work that make me think of poems, that make me think of techniques that a poet would use to make the language really resonate. Lots of prose, lots of fiction does this, but it's not a requirement necessarily; there's a fair amount of fiction widely distributed that doesn't really seem to have much interest in that at all. But that has been an experience of reading not just the novel that I've read of Karen's but also the letters [in the blog] have a kind of lyricism to them, a kind of singing quality that I've enjoyed so very much.

Work Cited

McElmurray, Karen Salyer, and Nancy Peacock. *Marginalia*. Nancy Peacock Books, 2014–2017.

PART 3

8

Still Holding at the Seams:
Magnolia Electric Co.'s *Josephine* and the
Contemporary Poetic Sequence

Contemporary poetry and independent roots music move through contemporary culture like two branches of the same river, with some common themes and concerns but with distinct ways of reaching their destinations. Each has been set adrift from their traditional methods and outlets of distribution, and both have found greater independence on the web and through new media but have also found a more diffuse marketplace. Both have small but dedicated followings that cross generational and cultural boundaries, and both exist on the fringes of larger economic entities that more or less neglect their existences. The deepest and most consequential bond, however, exists in the style and subject matter that make up the work of contemporary poetry and indie music. For example, listening to the 2007 release *The Stage Names* from the Austin, Texas, band Okkervil River and reading the 2005 poetry collection *The Book of Faces* by Joseph Campana present a strikingly similar set of qualities. In the same way that Okkervil River's album unfolds through a series of cinematic references and situations, beginning with the opening track "Our Life Is Not a Movie, or Maybe," Campana introduces the beguiling actress Audrey Hepburn, in a variety of real and imagined roles, as the muse of his poems. These two works, along with many others in recent years, seem to belong together less because of any common thematic bond than because of a loose structural coherence, a sense that their individual songs and poems make up a larger poetic sequence. One recent record, Magnolia Electric Co.'s 2009 release *Josephine*, stands in particularly close relation to contemporary poetry, both through its reliance on symbols and recurrent imagery as well as the sense that a definite, though incomplete, narrative holds the album together.

The poetic sequence provides poets with a solution to the question of how to expand on an image or occasion, without acquiescing to the inevitability of narrative resolution in prose fiction or to the historical and dramatic sweep of the epic. The sequence allows a poet to elaborate on an idea or sensation without necessarily telling a linear story about it. The sequence poem is not a recent development in American poetry. Interestingly, the roots of the genre trace back to the first distinctly, authoritatively American poetry, Walt Whitman's monumental *Leaves of Grass*. Whitman's poem *Song of Myself* makes a compelling case as a sequence of discreet lyrics, drawn together through the subjective qualities of perspective and sensibility, especially when compared against more traditional long poems such as William Wordsworth's *The Prelude* or John Milton's epic *Paradise Lost*. The contemporary lyric sequence bears at least one thing in common with Whitman's *Song of Myself*: the subject matter of the individual poems need not be the same to successfully carry the points of reference and connection through the entire piece.

Magnolia Electric Co. is a touring and recording collective of musicians led by singer and songwriter Jason Molina, and it began in 2003 after Molina retired his earlier band name, Songs: Ohia. The band plays a hybrid country/rock style reminiscent of Neil Young and Gram Parsons, solidly based out of the 1960s folk revival sound, a brand of music given a variety of names such as "alt-country" or "Americana." Like another highly literary singer-songwriter, Josh Ritter, Molina attended Oberlin College in Ohio. *Josephine* is the band's fifth album (and the first to pursue a clear sequence of songs), though Molina has released dozens of collaborations, side projects, and single/EP recordings. Not all the songs on *Josephine* are about the speaker's relationship with the character of Josephine, and many songs do not mention her at all. This distinguishes the album from earlier examples of song cycles, or "concept albums," in country and rock and roll music, such as Willie Nelson's classic *Red-Headed Stranger*, which tells the story of a wronged preacher who seeks revenge, and Neil Young's more recent *Greendale*, which documents the lives of a family of characters in a small California town. *Josephine* coheres because the emotional center of the songs revolves around the sense of loss that Josephine represents; even when she is not the direct subject, her absence is felt in the speaker's travels, and the mistakes that he has made in his life seem to lead back to their relationship.

The album's title track (and third song), addressed to Josephine, begins, "I turned your life so upside down / I don't know how you stayed, or why." He continues the verse by saying, "Looking always over my shoulder / Exactly what I was hoping to find was already mine. / Josephine, Josephine."[1] These lines establish both the speaker's mistreatment of his beloved and also his regret at his behavior. The following lines explain his actions: "But I saw the horizon, and I had to know where it all ends. / I lived so long with the shadows, Lord, I became one of them. / Oh, what a fool I've been, Josephine, Josephine."[2] The lines that shape the emotional center of the whole album come toward the end of the song, giving our best picture of Josephine's isolation and the speaker's regret: "You lock the door, and put them old records on / I hear you crying along / Oh, what a fool I've been."[3] The song ends with the speaker lamenting at how he tried to hold things together, but finally admitting that he followed the wrong dream, that he chased the horizon instead of showing his love for Josephine. The song doesn't resolve the situation but simply stakes a claim to be revisited throughout the album, ending with, "O Josephine / You are free / O Josephine."[4] Molina offers personal implications in the lyrics, but they are not quite confessional in the amount of detail revealed, and, as in much contemporary poetry, the distinction between the actual and the symbolic remains blurred.

If "Josephine" is the signal track on the album, the establishing shot for the whole sequence, then the song "Hope Dies Last" serves as a crux for all the threads running through the entire collection. The speaker's regret resurfaces when he scans his new landscape, retracing his steps: "I have mapped my falling sky from Harper's Ferry to the Gauley Bridge / Wichita

---

[1] Jason Molina, "Josephine," *Josephine*, Magnolia Electric Co., Secretly Canadian, 2009, CD.

[2] Ibid.

[3] Ibid.

[4] Ibid.

to Omaha, in the imminent bliss / but I made it too hard."[5] The song once again looks to the past—even the album's cover art (designed by Molina) suggests a world long departed, depicting a locket photograph woven into a lace doily of a young woman in nineteenth century dress. In a lovely unaccompanied duet, Molina sings with a backing vocalist, "I see the arrow climb, climb, climb / I know it finds my heart, every time."[6] The arrow in the heart reappears in the album's closing track, but in "Hope Dies Last" it reestablishes the pain and loss that drives the speaker's actions: "I make no small plans, my love / and I know hope dies last of all…Josephine, Josephine."[7] There is anguish in these lines, but not hopelessness, echoed again in the next song, "The Handing Down," with the lines, "Heart-worn more than most, I guess / But I'm still holding at the seams."[8] Josephine herself is not the only recurring element between songs on the album. Other motifs broaden the canvas, such as the wandering of the speaker, conveyed in "Map of the Falling Sky," and his pervasive loneliness, best seen in "Whip-Poor-Will," with its haunting refrain, "For all you people up in Heaven not too busy ringing the bell, / some of us down here ain't doing very well / some of us with our windows open in the Southern Cross Hotel."[9]

The album closes with "An Arrow in the Gale," another ode both to the speaker's time spent with Josephine and to life on the move. At only one minute, twenty-two seconds, one is tempted to call it a reprise of the earlier song "Josephine," yet the tone in this final track is much lighter, less bound to past mistakes, and more focused on the possibilities of the future. The opening lines are "Lightning on our tail, we gotta run, run, run / Lightning on our tail, we better go, Jo."[10] Even certain musical phrasings recur throughout the album, when chords and guitar lines repeat and in the background chant of "Run, run, run" later in the song, behind the lead vocal repeating the name "Josephine," both of which echo the title track and "Hope Dies Last." The final lines of the song present a question: "There's an arrow in the gale / and in the heartbeat / Oh, which one of us

---

[5] Jason Molina, "Hope Dies Last," *Josephine*.

[6] Ibid.

[7] Ibid.

[8] Jason Molina, "The Handing Down," *Josephine*.

[9] Jason Molina, "Whip-Poor-Will," *Josephine*.

[10] Jason Molina, "An Arrow in the Gale," *Josephine*.

is free, Josephine?"[11] The listener is left wondering about how to interpret this track as the album's conclusion: Is it a memory, a reunion; does it suggest a future with Josephine; or is it a look backward toward an intense moment they shared? The song, and the album as a whole, is as inconclusive as any lyric poem, or book of poems-in-sequence, and bears all the compression, imagery, and significant detail that characterize the best lyric poetry.

There are many examples in contemporary American writing of the poetic sequence, including some of the most celebrated volumes in recent memory. Louise Glück's Pulitzer Prize-winning collection *The Wild Iris* appeared in 1992, and its inventive use of a speaker in dialogue has made it one of the most discussed poetry books of that decade. Glück introduces a gardener who engages in parallel discussions with the flowers in her garden and with the voice of a god, all through a series of song-like lyrics in a sequence of recurring images and conceits. The Pulitzer Prize for Poetry was awarded to volumes that rely heavily on sequence poems in 2006, 2007, and 2010, respectively to Claudia Emerson's *Late Wife*, Natasha Trethewey's *Native Guard*, and Rae Armantrout's *Versed*. Emerson divides *Late Wife* into three sets of epistolary poems, each examining a different relationship and period of the speaker's life, culminating in a sequence of sonnets to her new husband about living with the death of his first wife. Trethewey also uses three sections for *Native Guard*, through which she intermingles personal trials, including the murder of her mother, with the historical situation of the Louisiana Native Guard, an all-Black regiment in the Civil War. Like Emerson, Trethewey displays a mastery of poetic forms, including the sonnet sequence that makes up the title poem. In *Versed*, Rae Armantrout, once known as a Language poet, employs a far more experimental sense of poetic style and a more fragmented set of experiences that are held together by an anxiety created by the speaker's illness. As these volumes indicate, the poetic sequence can take many shapes and styles as well as a variety of subject matter.

Larry Levis's posthumous collections of poems, *Elegy*, has become something of a touchstone for a younger generation of poets, a book that often comes up in conversations with a tone of awe at the accomplishment as well as a warmth that conveys real affection. More than any of the previously discussed books, *Elegy* folds its connections and linkages through

---

[11] Ibid.

the poems in a way that closely mirrors how the threads of recurrent imagery and thematic continuity are woven throughout *Josephine*. Even repetitions of various versions of elegy, the mode of poetry that mourns or
meditates upon the dead, create a sequential effect in the book. For example, Levis's poem "Anastasia and Sandman" introduces the image of the
horse and the holiness of the horse's natural state of being. The poem
opens with a scene:

> The brow of a horse in that moment when
> The horse is drinking water so deeply from a trough
> It seems to inhale the water, is holy.

> I refuse to explain.[12]

After this mysterious invocation, and the speaker's refusal to shed any
light on what it means, the poem forges the immediate scene, the water in
the trough, to its reflection of the infinite, the unknowable: "When the
horse had gone the water in the trough, / All through the empty summer,
/ Went on reflecting clouds & stars."[13] The poem proceeds through a rev-
erie addressed to "Members of the Committee on the Ineffable,"[14] then
into a bleak historical vision of Stalin's conquest of Romania, when he
confiscated the farmers' horses, leaving them with no means for tending
their land. Ultimately the species of the horse outlasts even Stalin's tyr-
anny, and ever present through the entire sequence is an angel lingering
beyond the fields, alighting in a horse's ear, and there is hope, three pages
later at the poem's conclusion, that good will prevail:

> I keep going to meetings where no one's there,
> And contributing to the discussion;
> And besides, behind the angel hissing in its mist
> Is a gate that leads only into another field,...[15]

---

[12] Larry Levis, "Anastasia and Sandman," in *Elegy* (Pittsburgh: University of
Pittsburgh Press, 1997), 8.
[13] Ibid., 8.
[14] Ibid., 8.
[15] Ibid., 8.

Here again the speaker uses indirection and seeming insignificance to guide the speaker of the poem into a deeper realization, where in fact the reader is introduced to the main players in the poem's drama, the title characters:

A horse named Sandman & a horse named Anastasia
Used to stand at the fence & watch the traffic pass.
Where there were outdoor concerts once, in summer,
Under the missing & innumerable stars.[16]

Levis establishes the significance of the horse, as well as the mystery of the stars, in "Anastasia and Sandman" and then revisits both symbols throughout *Elegy*. Other details, such as the significance of the year 1967 in the life of the poems' speaker, arise in several poems, but the horses, which appear on the book jacket in a kind of half-erased photographic negative image, are most central in the recurrent sequence. The two particular horses surface again, their relation to the speaker finally revealed, in a long poem from the third and final section of *Elegy*, titled "Elegy with the Sprawl of a Wave Inside It":

The wooden streets of MacLeod are lost in snow.

I love to say the names, over & over,
For the luster of their syllables, Vizcaino & Magellan,
Drake disappearing into mists off the Farallones.[17]

The speaker luxuriates over the language, the sound of names, before introducing the important figure of his grandmother:

Murrieta, Sontag & Evans, the Skeleton Club,

My grandmother Adah coming home after teaching school in a buggy
Drawn by the two horses, Anastasia & Sandman,

---

[16] Ibid., 8–9.
[17] Larry Levis, "Elegy with the Sprawl of a Wave Inside It," in *Elegy*, 44.

A small Derringer with a pearl handle in her lap.[18]

All of this hardly prepares us for the poem's actual resolution, which involves the speaker's father and his unexpected return to his home.

My father walking halfway over the swaying bridge
Of the last whaling boat—

Bound for Juneau out of San Francisco Bay &
Then turning around in the middle, deciding not to.[19]

Anastasia and Sandman also appear in the later poem "Elegy with a Bridle in Its Hand," which presents the speaker's memory of riding the two aged horses when he was a boy. The pervasive, but never openly revealed, significance of the horses in *Elegy* mirrors the elusiveness of the character of Josephine and the unresolved nature of her relationship with the speaker of Magnolia Electric Co.'s songs about her.

Given the relative predominance of the form, surprisingly little criticism has been written about the lyric sequence. The most wide-ranging study on the subject was published in 1983, *The Modern Poetic Sequence: The Genius of Modern Poetry* by M. L. Rosenthal and Sally Gall. In the section of their introductory chapter, titled "The 'New' Genre and Organic Form," Rosenthal and Gall consider how the sequence emerges into its own:

> Its presence becomes abundantly obvious, for the modern sequence is the decisive form toward which all developments of modern poetry have tended. It is the genre which best encompasses the shift in sensibility exemplified by starting a long poetic work "I celebrate myself, and sing myself," rather than "Sing, Goddess, the wrath of Achilles." The modern sequence goes many-sidedly into who and where we are *subjectively* [emphasis in original]; it springs from the same pressures on sensibility that have caused our poets' experiments with shorter forms. It, too, is a response to the lyrical possibilities of language opened up by those pressures in times of cultural

---

[18] Ibid., 44.
[19] Ibid., 44.

and psychological crisis, when all past certainties have many times been thrown chaotically into question. More successfully than individual short lyrics, however, it fulfills the need for encompassment of disparate and often powerfully opposed tonalities and energies.[20]

As with other elements of style and structure in poetry, the sequence as mapped out by Rosenthal and Gall has evolved since the period of High Modernist triumph. A reconsideration of how the sequence poem functions now is long overdue. One clear modification over time is that the kind of material that creates a thread of continuity throughout the poem is less overt; the connections are fainter, more subtly construed. The dominant themes in such monolithic poetry as T. S. Eliot's *The Waste Land*, Ezra Pound's *The Cantos*, and William Carlos Williams's *Paterson* announce themselves with a clarity that unifies even disparate parts of the works. These poems are all part of the "American Flowering" of the new genre, which according to Rosenthal and Gall expands on the promise of Whitman's experiments. In contrast, the unifying elements in Levis's *Elegy*, as well as in Magnolia Electric Co.'s *Josephine*, lie buried in images or correspondences between images. The linking thread that generates coherence in these recent works forms something more like a trail (a "fading trail," to echo an earlier Magnolia Electric Co. album title) than a highway system.

During the week of the album's release, Pitchfork.tv ran a full-length documentary called *Recording Josephine*, in which filmmaker Ben Schreiner observed the band during the recording of the album. Much of the film focuses on in-studio details of how individual songs go through different versions, along with interview segments with the band and their near-legendary producer Steve Albini. Near the end of the documentary, however, Schreiner finally asks Jason Molina, the band's singer and songwriter, about the lyrics for the record. Molina is coy, even evasive, about what the songs refer to, and like any true poet he seems unwilling to commit the "heresy of paraphrase." Just as he becomes visibly uncomfortable, on the verge of saying something definite, the camera makes an abrupt cut, which signals the end of the film. The band could not have been more forthcoming about the process of recording their instruments, but when it came to discussing lyrics, the secret could not be unveiled. As in a fine sequence of

---

[20] M. L. Rosenthal and Sally Gall, *The Modern Poetic Sequence: The Genius of Modern Poetry* (Oxford: Oxford University Press, 1983), 3.

poems, following the thread of images and implications as it winds through *Josephine* gives all the joy, and the satisfaction, of a mystery not quite revealed.

9

Waltzing through the *Mysterium*: The Evolving Role of Music in the Poetry of David Bottoms

Several times through the years, David Bottoms has put forth metaphors for the way poetry works and for how he writes his own poems. One example stands out: that of the "poet as radio," as a receiver for the offerings of the world, and as a transmitter of the messages received.[1] Bottoms has gone on record calling it his "corniest" metaphor for how writing happens, but the radio is, in fact, an apt analogy for Bottoms's poetry, if not necessarily for the poet himself. The radio serves as the carrier of an invisible history, sent forth by waves that might appear to defy time and space, in much the way that memory, the great *mysterium* in Bottoms's poetry, emanates from unseen sources. The presence of music as a storehouse for images and recollections appears consistently in every volume of Bottoms's poetry, but the role it plays changes considerably from his early work to his later work. In the early poems, music serves primarily as a point of reference and helps establish a scene for the portrayal of an event. In more recent poems, however, music has gone beyond a trigger for memory and

---

[1] Alice Friman and Bruce Gentry, "Fishing from the Poetry Boat: A Conversation with David Bottoms," *The Southern Quarterly* 37, nos. 3–4 (1999): 100.

has become a guide or a talisman in the search for meaning. Music functions as a means of transport and transcendence, a way to get closer to the hidden essences of truth and to give the speakers of the poems a more expansive vision of the world.

Bottoms's first volume of poems, *Shooting Rats at the Bibb County Dump*, won the prestigious Walt Whitman Award from the Academy of American Poets in 1979. The book was selected for the award by Robert Penn Warren, who, in his introduction to the book, found in Bottoms "a strong poet, and much of his strength emerges from the fact that he is temperamentally a realist. In his vision the actual world is not transformed but illuminated."[2] Such an endorsement by Warren signaled a passing of the torch in Southern poetry. Bottoms follows in the lineage of Southern poets that dates back to Sydney Lanier but that most prominently features Warren and James Dickey. This line of influence follows such themes as an individual person's communion with nature; focus on memories from childhood; and the search for spiritual consolation in a world that appears indifferent but rich in meaning. Dave Smith notes a similar thread in Bottoms's work: "In the historic male and rural vision of the South, a man fishes, hunts, knows the creatures, acclimates himself to what is beyond the momentary, and even the cyclical; he seeks to know and acknowledge what is permanent, a divinity more Calvinist than redemptive. This is core Agrarian thinking...."[3] Bottoms's work, however, does not rest in that comfortable core of the Agrarian mindset. Bottoms is a poet of contemporary life and does not settle for nostalgic backward glances, and while he is deeply reflective on the significance of the past, his poems consistently engage the world as it must be lived in during the present. Writing about playing music, or watching it performed, is one of the ways Bottoms evokes life in the moment. Through poems such as "Jamming with the Band at the VFW" and "Writing on Napkins at the Sunshine Club" in *Shooting Rats at the Bibb County Dump* from 1980, and "O Mandolin, O Magnum Mysterium" and "Vigilance" in *Waltzing through the Endtime* from 2004, Bottoms shows the essential necessity of paying due attention to the events and situations at hand.

---

[2] Robert Penn Warren, back cover of David Bottoms, *Shooting Rats at the Bibb County Dump* (New York: Morrow, 1980).

[3] Dave Smith, "The Vigilant Words of David Bottoms," in *David Bottoms: Critical Essays and Interviews*, ed. William Walsh (Jefferson, NC: McFarland & Co. Publishers, 2010), 16.

One of Bottoms's most well-known early poems is "Jamming with the Band at the VFW," in which the speaker observes a dance floor scene from a table, his true identity tucked under his cowboy hat, before suddenly finding himself drawn into the action. The poem is typical of his work from this period, a set piece under thirty lines in length, directed by a poet's watchful eye, driven by resonate observations of other peoples' behaviors, until the end of the poem, when he rises and makes himself vulnerable:

> Then rising from my chair
> I drank the last of the Pabst
> and moved through the bruised light of the bandstand
> onto the purple dance floor, toward the tables
> across the room, toward the table beside the bar,
> and there the woman with platinum hair
> and rhinestone earrings, moving suddenly toward me.[4]

The music in this poem, as in its companion piece, "Writing on Napkins at the Sunshine Club," provides more than simply a backdrop and a reason for being in the particular setting. Listening to the "tear-jerking music" makes the speaker think of "all my written words, / all the English classes, the workshops"[5] that have become the work of his life and that might render him an outsider at the VFW, where he otherwise feels so much at home. What prevents this scene from becoming merely sentimental self-reflection is Bottoms's remarkable and persistent capacity to enlarge the scope of his experiences. Rather than linger on thoughts of his own successes and disappointments, his speaker moves immediately back to the men on the dance floor, possible older versions of himself who "dream of having died / at Anzio, Midway, Guadalcanal." The speaker in "Jamming with the Band at the VFW" weighs these lives against the "arty sophisticates" he knows in Atlanta, takes the measure of the old men's dreams and their sacrifices, and finds a valuable truthfulness in them.

A reader enters the early poetry of David Bottoms as one might ap-

---

[4] David Bottoms, "Jamming with the Band at the VFW," in *Shooting Rats at the Bibb County Dump*, 15.

[5] Bottoms, "Writing on Napkins at the Sunshine Club," in *Shooting Rats at the Bibb County Dump*, 28.

proach a novel by Thomas Hardy, with the certainty of event and consequence. The same element of chance that haunts the characters in *The
Return of the Native* or *The Mayor of Casterbridge*, what the great master
called "hap," looms over the inhabitants of most Bottoms poems. As in
Hardy, motives for action may remain murky, but the resolutions of the
early poems are definite, though their meanings are never made overly explicit. Many of Bottoms's most-discussed early poems, such as the title
poem to *Shooting Rats at the Bibb County Dump* and "Under the Boat-
house," from his second collection *In a U-Haul North of Damascus*, resolve
in ways that suggest a type of coherence within experience, a should-have-
known-better resignation about human intentions. The resolution in Bottoms's later poems may be less direct, but they maintain a Hardy-esque
attention to the unknowable, or unforeseeable, aspect of human experience.

Bottoms is most often discussed as a narrative poet, and that is primarily accurate, especially in the earlier part of his career. Bottoms's poems
frequently evoke memories from the speaker's past, but they rarely deliver
a straightforward plot with the usual elements of fiction; more often the
poems use memories to examine some unseen aspect of the mind's steady
unfolding in response to an incident. To a large degree, how the events are
remembered and how their meaning is made becomes more significant
than the events themselves. In an essay about Fred Chappell, another
poet/novelist from the South, Robert Morgan claims, "What Chappell
does best is what may be termed *lyric narrative*,[6] implying that the local
texture of the lines is as interesting and concise as lyric poetry, while the
overall movement of each piece is essentially narrative."[7] This view can be
usefully applied to Bottoms's later poetry, which works on a larger canvas
than the lyric poem usually permits, yet moves poems along through observations and meditations that are lyric in their natures. Morgan makes
an additional formal distinction between verse and prose: "The difference
between prose narrative and verse narrative is considerable: the former

---

[6] Edward Byrne uses this same term in a fine overview essay on Bottoms's
poetry. Though Byrne does not offer an extended definition of the concept, as
Morgan does, I interpret the usage to be synonymous.

[7] Robert Morgan, "*Midquest* and the Gift of Narrative," in *Dream Garden:
The Poetic Vision of Fred Chappell*, ed. Patrick Bizzaro (Baton Rouge: LSU Press,
1996), 133–34.

usually incorporates much more detail and proceeds at the pace of the reader; the latter leaves far more to implication, as in other verse, and proceeds at the slower rhythm of repeated lineation."[8] The "implication" Morgan speaks of can be expanded to include "ambiguity" in Bottoms's poetry as well as "indirection" and "suggestion," all of which are seen with much greater frequency in his later work.

The evolving role of music bears an intimate connection between Bottoms's move away from closed narratives and toward more expansive and ambiguous meditations. Form follows the lead of content in this case, and as the content takes on a deeper search for meaning, the form must loosen enough to allow a layering, a scaffolding effect, to develop. The turning point in this direction comes in the middle of Bottoms's 1999 volume *Vagrant Grace*, with the poem "Country Store and Moment of Grace." The poem is eighteen pages long, and it stands out among a collection of tightly structured dramatic poems. Though "Country Store and Moment of Grace" still follows a narrative line, the extended study of the ways of life associated with the scene gives the poem an exploratory quality not available in shorter lyrics. Charles Wright's mid- and later-career poetry would seem to be an influence here, both in terms of form and content, which seems to have opened a whole new avenue of inquiry for Bottoms in both the shape and scope of a lyric poem. Wright's influence has been pervasive since the late 1980s, with poets as varied as Larry Levis, Forrest Gander, Tom Andrews, David St. John, Judy Jordan, and many others emulating to great effect Wright's inventive use of line and measure. Wright began in his 1981 collection *The Southern Cross* to move away from the obliqueness of his earlier poems, developing a *new narrative* sensibility that continues to resonate in American poetry, particularly with writers who come from the South. In the case of Bottoms, the form of his poems flexes and allows for a more comprehensive approach to his subject matter.

"O Mandolin, *O Magnum Mysterium*" is one of the most ambitious poems in *Waltzing through the Endtime*, and it also provides one of the clearest examples of the evolving role music plays in Bottoms's poetry. The poem opens with the speaker's first encounter with the instrument in a junkshop, a setting that might evoke a scene from Ingmar Bergman's film *Fanny and Alexander*, the air filled with mystery that the speaker downplays:

[8] Ibid., 134.

Ah, the music of the spheres, the old Jew quipped, plowing his walker
down the pawnshop aisle.
Whatever, I nod,
and cradle the beautifully scarred mandolin in my open palms—
rutted ebony fingerboard, caramel-grained face of rusty spruce,
two strings missing, bridge cracked.[9]

The speaker's first response is skepticism, but there is also an immediate
connection with the instrument's own suffering, its own difficult passage
into his open hands.

Torture, I thought, teaching myself
to play this thing, then pondered all the other agonies
it must have endured—
the lovers wooed and lost, the bottles dodged
in barroom discourses,
loneliness of widowers on their porches at night,
their hard music rising in starlight.[10]

The mandolin is a conduit for the suffering of those who have played it,
and with a single note the speaker hears its imperfection and also finds its
analogue in nature:

String pluck and fret buzz—the sound of a spooked bird.

I turn to the window to read through the dust its history in scars,
my face, no doubt, the mug of a doubter.
So what, pleads the pawnbroker,
you'll have the mystery.[11]

The pawnbroker is selling more than a faulty old instrument. He
promises access to something wondrous; the speaker, however, hears the
word *misery* in the old man's plea. The meditation of the poem enlarges at

---

[9] Bottoms, "O Mandolin, *O Magnum Mysterium,*" in *Waltzing through the
Endtime* (Port Townsend, WA: Copper Canyon, 2004), 7.
[10] Ibid.
[11] Ibid.

this point, taking in the speaker's associations with human misery, accompanied always by the mandolin. He takes the mandolin out to the riverbank to play, and he muses upon a jogger passing by, then a neighbor he once had in Georgia ("Steppenwolf in Macon? Playing Mozart on the Mandolin?"). His thoughts move back and forth between these two unlikely figures until he recalls the implied suicide of the drunken neighbor. Always skeptical, the speaker recalls Coleridge's *Viper thoughts* and cannot get the suffering of others out of his mind as his mandolin playing provides a soundtrack for such musings. The poem concludes, after five pages, with the jogger's return to the riverbank and his obliviousness to the water moccasin that swims toward him. Of the snake, the speaker says, "black as a tree root, glistening, / its beauty a witness to the world's sense of irony," which is also the irony of the mandolin, through which pain and misery give way to beautiful expression, to a true articulation of the human spirit.

Music is a figurative mode of expression and must evoke its message through association. This is especially true when the music is not accompanied by lyrics. The mandolin is always played solo in *Waltzing through the Endtime*, songs without words to convey their emotions. In the poem "Black Hawk Rag," the speaker searches for the right mode to express "the rhythms of memory":

> All morning by the kitchen window
> prowling the neck of the mandolin for the misplaced notes of a tune—
> big wind after cold rain
>   and half the leaves on the sugar maple have
> tumbled
> onto the wet grass. The mandolin whines like it wants to fly south.[12]

The tune is one the speaker's grandfather used to play in the garage by his old store, and by trying to find its notes, the speaker searches not only for a song but for the memory of his grandfather. This poem echoes "O Mandolin, O *Magnum Mysterium*" in its use of music, and particularly the playing of the mandolin, as a way of engaging with the past, even a transport through time. The poem's conclusion demonstrates the interesting possibility, or the speaker's wish, that recapturing the elusive notes of

---

[12] Bottoms, "Black Hawk Rag," in *Waltzing through the Endtime*, 51.

the grandfather's song would someday bring the two of them back together:

> Silly to lean on the rhythms of memory,
> Which will hardly give back
>   Even the threads of that rag. But what else
> To suggest he's still in that garage, hunched
> In a shadow, fiddle
> Under chin, waiting for my ghost to swing through the door?[13]

"Black Hawk Rag" is less expansive than some of Bottoms's work
from this period, but it shares many concerns with the longer pieces, including that the mind develops connections through imagery and that
sound imagery can be just as vital as visual triggers or other sensory perceptions. Even Nature takes part in this musical interchange, as in "Melville in the Bass Boat," where the speaker's mind drifts "Over the blending
rhythms of water and word."[14] This rich image intertwines Nature and
language, with the suggestion being that words are as fluid as water, and
the intimate bond between them relies on the musical element of rhythm.

In his memoir, *Another Beauty*, Polish poet Adam Zagajewski often
writes about music as a means of accessing the past. He recalls concert
performances he has seen by listening to recordings of the compositions;
he reflects on individual composers, at one point considering the irony that
Bach fathered twenty children, while his celebrated interpreter, Glenn
Gould, committed himself to isolation in order to devote his life to Bach's
work. At one point, Zagajewski asks, "What is the link between music and
poetry?" His answer is startlingly brief and simple: "Poetry."[15] Zagajewski
implies the necessity of poetry's contribution to the architectural abstrac-
tion of music, assigning poetry the primary role in the relationship. This
idea runs parallel to the way David Bottoms employs music as a tool for
exploration into the historical and metaphysical concerns of his poetry. In
an interview with William Walsh, Bottoms says, "What I am trying to
unravel is sort of the ultimate reason for everything and as Warren said,

---

[13] Ibid.

[14] Bottoms, "Melville in the Bass Boat," in *Waltzing through the Endtime*, 37.

[15] Adam Zagajewski, *Another Beauty* (Athens: UGA Press, 2002.), 76.

'the logic behind the original dream.' But, you know you are not going to be able to do that because you didn't dream the original dream. You are only a part of it, which is an interesting irony, and yet, there is something that compels you to keep searching."[16] This quote hints at the spiritual search inherent in Bottoms's later expansive work, the sense that if the right memories are brought into alignment, some meaning of the past will become clear and perhaps some ultimate truth will be revealed.

Bottoms often pays tribute to his favorite musicians in poems, naming them and occasionally referring to signature songs or lyrics. One of the more searching poems in *Waltzing through the Endtime* is "In the Big House of the Allman Brothers My Heart Gets Tuned." The Allman Brothers are local legends in Bottoms's part of Georgia, and the poem plays out an early association the speaker has with their childhood home, while also keeping an eye on his present situation. "In the Big House..." is also a multi-page, multi-section piece that begins with a meditation on sleep and dreams and being a visitor in a strange house that once belonged to his musical heroes. The poem then recalls an episode from twenty-eight years earlier in the speaker's life, when he once stood outside that same house where he is now a guest and listened to the band practicing from within. The younger version of the speaker was strung out on drugs and hoping for some sign of divinity or spiritual transcendence, all of which is mirrored in the older self of the speaker, who nervously considers whether the ghosts of the two deceased band members might be stirring in the house with him:

> No, neither touching a string, though something is playing the bones
> of this house—strung out memory
> or middle-aged panic—
>   as I listen near the corner of sleep
> to the heating pipes, to the floor beams and roof beams shifting
> toward the rhythm of my breath,
>   as though the house,
> my heartbeat, the larger night, were all tuning up for the lifting
> of some curtain,

---

[16] William Walsh, "The Logic of the Original Dream: An Interview with David Bottoms," in *David Bottoms: Critical Essays and Interviews*, 126.

the way one guitar will lean toward another
in those final, unnerving moments
of rehearsal...[17]

Once again, music is the medium for transport, or for signal, from a spiritual realm. Even the breath of the speaker conforms to the musical element of rhythm, and his heartbeat colludes with the house and the night itself to be tuned, like an instrument, so that it may receive a vision from beyond the lifted veil. Music resides among the mystical elements in Bottoms's poetry, though it travels freely between the bodily and the ethereal, connecting the two in ways that are not available by other means, making contact "down there / where the spirit meets the bone,"[18] to quote Miller Williams, another Southern poet with deep musical affiliations.

The title *Waltzing through the Endtime* comes from a phrase in the book's final poem, "Three-Quarter Moon and Moment of Grace," and is uttered by the speaker, who recalls it as his mother-in-law's saying. The mandolin figures into this poem as well, as the speaker walks across his darkened yard under the watchful, "pocked eye" of the moon, "where a middle aged man, playing mandolin, / limps barefoot through his yard, / barefoot and grateful."[19] The gratitude is undefined, possibly felt for the simple opportunity to do this kind of soul-searching. The next lines reveal the book's title: "*Waltzing through the Endtime*, my mother-in-law calls it, / wringing out my spirit like a dirty dishrag."[20] This line conveys a kind of sardonic wisdom from the older woman, who shared her dream of riding through a flood on a floating outhouse that closes the previous poem, "Vigilance." Waltzing is an off-kilter, wavering dance, with the original Austrian version performed in three-quarter time, which resonates with the poem's title. It also resonates with the speaker's approach to seeking wisdom, which is through worry and fret, back and forth, always looking out for a sign that could easily be missed.

---

[17] Bottoms, "In the Big House of the Allman Brothers My Heart Gets Tuned," in *Waltzing through the Endtime*, 19.

[18] Miller Williams, "Compassion," in *The Ways We Touch* (Champaign: University of Illinois Press, 1997), 55.

[19] Bottoms, "Three-Quarter Moon and Moment of Grace," in *Waltzing through the Endtime*, 58.

[20] Ibid.

The mandolin makes a curious and fitting emblem of the talisman that Bottoms follows throughout *Waltzing through the Endtime.* It is less pervasive and popularized than the guitar or the violin but offers the same range of musical genre affiliations. With both classical and folk origins, the mandolin has recently become popular in American bluegrass music. The waltz and the mandolin both have European origins, the same cultural roots as the mysticism that also informs Bottoms's search for the meaning in memories of past times. Both the waltz and the mandolin have established a presence in the folk and popular music of the American South, especially in the rural cultures of the middle twentieth century, which occupies so much of Bottoms's imaginative space.

In 2011, Bottoms published his ninth collection of poems, *We Almost Disappear.* The poems in this volume occasionally address music, and in such examples as "Love at the Sunshine Club" and "Bluesman Home from a Cherry Street Bar," musical imagery steers the content of the poems. These are short lyric poems, in a book composed mainly of brief poems of deep illumination, and they lack the expansive range of "O Mandolin, O *Magnum Mysterium.*" Many of the poems focus intently on the aging of the poet's father, which is a different and more concrete form of change than Bottoms has pursued before. Thus, the poems are no less meditative than in his other recent work, but their scope is more restrained. While music still plays a role in the volume, it more closely resembles the role it played in earlier works, less a mode of transport and more an element of atmosphere and description. The poem from *We Almost Disappear* that most recalls the searching quality of Bottoms's other later work involving music is "A Cello Bird," in which the speaker listens to his daughter practicing her instrument:

> She leans forward, shoulders curled, and the shadows
> streaking the patio blend girl
> and cello into one clumsy bird—bent neck, hooked beak, one wing
> flapping.
>
> Before long the trees sing back.
>
> When I was a boy I, too, wanted to become a bird
> and, day after day,
> whistled through the scrub woods behind our

house.[21]

Once again, the performing of music, the playing of an instrument, is a transformative experience, different from simply listening to recorded music. The conclusion of "A Cello Bird" shows as clearly as any Bottoms poem the power music has to remake the world:

> Who knows how she charms those tiny voices out of the dark
> and keeps them singing
> in the yard? Who knows how far they travel?
>
> > Or where
> she's planning to go
> all dressed up in that plumage of shadow.[22]

The speaker of the poem is left with more questions than answers, though they are questions of delight and not of worry or dread. The speaker is content to live in the *negative capability* required by the moment, in which he cannot understand his daughter's communion with Nature, but he also feels no need to pursue, to reach after, any further explanation for it.

Strong poets demonstrate a dynamic range of voice and a varied array of content that evolves as their work matures. David Bottoms has proven himself to be one of America's strongest poets, ever expanding his storehouse of materials and searching out new depths in his individual pursuit of a meaningful understanding of life. Though Bottoms moves increasingly between distinctive narrative and meditative lyric modes, his poems are always experiential, always embodying what happens to and around the speaker. Bottoms has appeared less interested in adopting character personas in his recent work, relying instead on a singular consistent voice, ostensibly autobiographical, and developing the full scope of one man's life. Throughout his career, music has facilitated or represented aspects of this life in his poetry, and it has taken on an increasingly significant role as a trigger for memory and association. Music, and particularly the playing of an instrument, gives voice to feelings and intuitions that cannot be

---

[21] Bottoms, "A Cello Bird," in *We Almost Disappear* (Port Townsend, WA: Copper Canyon, 2011), 28.

[22] Ibid., 28.

expressed in words, and it can become a means for spiritual transcendence. If the analogy of the "poet as radio" does not fully represent the poet's role, it does offer an insight into how meaning gets delivered. In David Bottoms's poetry, the quest for meaning is not resolved through conventional avenues, and searching for expression through music offers a new portal into the great realm: the *mysterium* where the past, the spirit, and the fate of the individual self align into a unified field of vision.

10

The Single Seam in *The Double Dream of Spring:* John Ashbery's Natural Sublime

As the rich and controversial public life of John Ashbery's poetry settles into its sixth decade—his volume *Some Trees* won the 1956 Yale Younger Poets Prize—the time seems right to consider some of its underappreciated aspects. An examination of the iconography of John Ashbery's full body of work reveals that nothing so predominates as the imagery of natural landscapes. This alone fails to distinguish Ashbery from a number of his major contemporaries, such as W. S. Merwin, Charles Wright, or Louise Glück, but Ashbery's approach to natural environments (a separate argument could contend man-made environments as well) differs dramatically from that of other important poets of his generation. In so many ways, Ashbery works against prevailing usages and meanings when addressing the natural world, though its appearance plays no less crucial a role in his work than in that of other poets more closely affiliated with it. The central condition of Ashbery's poetry may be dislocation, a sense of unstable meanings and frames of reference in which the possibility for misrecognition or incompletion creates a feeling of uncertainty in the poem's speaker, and in the reader as well. Since Ashbery does not write confessional or typically representational poetry, images of natural objects, and the meanings usually attached to them, contribute to and compound the

effect of dislocation: not only does the speaker have a disjunctive relationship to the language of his own experience, but the most static figures in
the external world—trees, rivers, the ground itself—seem capable of
movement, of slippage out of the context in which we have come to know
them. One important effect of this decentering process emerges in the
form of sublime recovery, as the image refuses to yield a comforting or
familiar meaning, and understanding must be sought in some "other tradition," to employ a favorite phrase of Ashbery's, some other means for
comprehension.

The idea of the sublime dates back to the ancient Greeks and in particular to a study of rhetorical technique titled *On the Sublime*, attributed
to a philosopher named Longinus, who believed that language could convey the sublime through emotional intensity and sweep. Definitions of the
sublime evolve throughout the eighteenth and nineteenth centuries in literature and art, but certain qualities remain constant, such as the promise
of man's transcendence above the human condition, the presence of mystery and vastness in the experience of sublimity, and the alignment of
beauty and terror that characterizes the fallen angels in Milton's *Paradise
Lost*. Important distinctions exist as to whether the sublime originates in
man, in nature, or from a divine interlocutor, as well as distinctions between the sublime, the beautiful, and the picturesque, not to mention the
ridiculous, which stands as a sort of alter ego to the sublime. Another consistent attribute of the sublime is a feeling of disorientation or confusion
in the face of the sublime object, occasionally followed by a recovery of
equilibrium that brings with it an enlarged sense of understanding or insight. Ashbery's interest in sublimity is, like the Romantics, experiential
and worldly, unlike Immanuel Kant, who believed that such a response is
preconditioned in the mind of the observer, and more like Edmund Burke,
whose ideas are discussed in a later paragraph. When the speaker in an
Ashbery poem encounters a sublime instance in nature, it likely arrives in
the form of some small or unexpected detail or occurrence, and this inver-
sion of the vastness associated with the concept distinguishes his recognition of sublimity and gives it a decidedly postmodern character. While
Ashbery's approach toward the sublime in nature originates with the British Romantic poets, it more resembles the enigmatic, lesser-known rever-
ies of John Clare than the meditative and expansive musings of William
Wordsworth.

Ashbery's fourth volume of poems, *The Double Dream of Spring*, published in 1970, marks a change in both the surface appearance and the intellectual undercurrent of the poet's work, and it stands out in hindsight as a point of significant change of focus in an already accomplished career. One aspect of the transition *The Double Dream of Spring* registered was a move away from the abrupt French-inspired dislocations of the speaker and from the harshly transposed juxtapositions of thought and image that characterized Ashbery's earlier collections, *Some Trees* and *The Tennis Court Oath*. In *The Double Dream of Spring*, Ashbery moves toward a longer verse line and increasingly meditative passages, wherein thoughts can be sustained and reflected against other thoughts or images rather than snipped elliptically from their initial directions, as in the earlier works. This lengthening of observation allows for an underpinning to develop beneath the poems' widely varied tones, forms, and attitudes, a single seam of recognition, a constant pull between the promise of the natural sublime and a persistent undercutting of sublime recovery, implying a self capacious enough to incorporate the contradictions of modern life. Ashbery manages to find a source of sustenance there without denying the limitations that circumscribe human experience, and he finds a kind of sublime recovery in a patient and persistent attention to the details of experience, no matter how changeable and deceptive those may be.

The sense of sources having lost their meanings, and frames of reference existing without necessary contexts, provides the opening situation of the poem "Summer," from *The Double Dream of Spring*:

There is that sound like the wind
Forgetting in the branches that means something
Nobody can translate. And there is the sobering "later on,"
When you consider what a thing meant, and put it down.[1]

Ashbery frequently employs the language of pastoral poetry, as in the simile of "that sound like the wind," and even personifies it by having it perform functions of the human mind—to forget, to make meaning. Given the book's title and the titles and images of so many of its poems, one might be tempted to call Ashbery a pastoralist, but he clearly resists

---

[1] John Ashbery, "Summer," in *The Double Dream of Spring* (New York: Dutton, 1970), 20.

the pastoral impulse if we regard the sense in which William Empson uses the term, as in a comparison of the simple life with the complex life, with advantage shown to the simple. Ashbery refuses both comparison and advantage, as both imply a measure of Kantian reason and order that Ashbery denies, just as he refuses the application of an external clarity for an internal confusion.

Instead of a version of pastoralism, however, what John Ashbery discovers in "Summer" is a version of the natural sublime. Where the poem does not allow an endorsement of the "simple life"—indeed would not even grant that such a life exists—given that our own observations of the external world are "sobering" in their uncertainty, it does permit a moment of recognition, though not a soft one:

> And the thinning-out phase follows
> The period of reflection. And suddenly, to be dying
> Is not a little or mean or cheap thing,
> Only wearying, the heat unbearable,
>
> And also the little mindless construction put upon
> Our fantasies of what we did: summer, the ball of pine needles
> The loose fates serving our acts, with token smiles,
> Carrying out their instructions too accurately—
>
> Too late to cancel them now—and winter, the twitter
> Of cold stars at the pane, that describes with broad gestures
> This state of being that is not so big after all.[2]

The landscape in this passage works as a lever toward understanding, despite its indirection and seeming randomness. The moment of sublimity here begins in the untranslatable quality of the message in the trees, perhaps the remnants of belief in a divine presence, a meaning that the creation of Nature proves, but the sublimity also reaches into the incompleteness of putting it all down. This could easily be a paralyzing sensation for a poet, the knowledge that considering "what a thing meant" is an artifice at best and a self-delusion at worst. The moment of dejection is casually stated as "Too late to cancel them now—," as though the experiences were

---

[2] Ibid., 20.

regrettable, but not more so than having written a bad check or having ordered the wrong dessert after dinner. Despite Ashbery's typical de-emphasizing tone, the consequence of the observation loses no significance, as the state of being, and the eventual certainty of not-being, emerges as the poem's true subject.

One might complain that "Summer" could just as easily be read as merely an exercise in the sort of frustrating evasion of which Ashbery is so frequently accused. Isn't it possible that the entire gesture of the poem is an ironic commentary on the uselessness and sentimentality of looking for meanings that relate one's life to one's death? Isn't one event just as random as the other? It might seem particularly ridiculous to listen for messages in the wind as it blows through the trees, but that joke begins and ends in the first stanza of the poem, as the question of death emerges in the shadow dispersed among the trees in the forest, just as life is "divided up / Between you and me, and among all the others out there."[3] Ashbery is no nihilist, any more than he is simply a prankster or a purveyor only of language games. In her book, *Shifting Ground: Reinventing Landscape in Modern American Poetry*, Bonnie Costello draws a distinction between Ashbery's poetics and what Fredric Jameson calls "the detached spatiality"[4] that determines the condition of postmodernity:

> Landscape is, rather, a fundamental, generating trope of knowledge in Ashbery's poetry, I believe, because it insistently invokes an observer and his environment and draws out assumptions of knowledge within our everyday accounts of what we know. Ashbery's poetry sets out to present the feeling of our contemporary landscape of knowledge—unsteady, even cataclysmic, full of trompe l'oeil and obscurities, but occasionally luminous. His work remains deeply tied to the meditative tradition of landscape reverie and allegory from Dante to Stevens.[5]

As Costello points out in her metaphor of knowledge appearing as a landscape, Ashbery accepts contradictions in the contemporary search for meaning, comfortable with not knowing what lies behind the trees in a

---

[3] Ibid., 8.

[4] Fredric Jameson, *Postmodernism; or, The Cultural Logic of Late Capitalism* (Durham: Duke University Press, 1991), 185.

[5] Bonnie Costello, *Shifting Ground: Reinventing Landscape in Modern American Poetry* (Cambridge: Harvard University Press, 2003), 175.

forest, with shadows concealing potential danger and delusion. This acceptance is one of many traits that place Ashbery in the Whitmanic line of American poetry, and an inhabiting of the natural sublime stands as an extension of that refusal to be denied value and significance. The concluding lines of "Summer" indicate the type of sublime recompense a skeptical seeker might experience:

Summer involves going down a steep flight of steps

To a narrow ledge over the water. Is this it, then,
This iron comfort, these reasonable taboos,
Or did you mean it when you stopped? And the face
Resembles yours, the one reflected in the water.[6]

In Ashbery's poetry, instances of the natural sublime occur in less monumental forms than in the work of British Romantic poets, for whom the vastness of the Alps offered the definitive image of Nature's sublimity, its dominance over human life, and also, as in the case of Wordworth's Simplon Pass episode from *The Prelude*, the surprise by which it can overwhelm the human mind. Perhaps the most illustrative example of the effect of the Romantic version of the natural sublime appears in Shelley's "Mont Blanc," with lines that read, "Dizzy ravine! and when I gaze on thee / I seem as in a trance sublime and strange...." Shelley goes on in the passage to situate his speaker's mind as passively attuned to his surroundings yet overwhelmed by "one legion of wild thoughts" brought on by the magnitude of the landscape. In Ashbery's work, however, magnitude is no longer required from natural settings to produce sublime effects. In fact, no aspect of living requires magnitude to achieve the sublime, as the unexpected and unexplained "surge" in the following passage from "Sortes Vergilianae" demonstrates:

Lately you've found the dull fever still inflict their round, only they are
    unassimilable
Now that newness or importance has worn away. It is with us like
    day and
  night,

---

[6] Ashbery, "Summer," 20.

120

The surge upward through grade-school positioning and bursting into
   soft gray blooms
Like vacuum cleaner sweepings, the opulent fuzz of our cage, or like an
   excited insect
In nervous scrimmage for the head, etching its none-too-complex
   ordinances into the matter of the day.[7]

Ashbery invokes the name of Vergil, the great Roman poet of the
pastoral, while he establishes the union of beauty and terror that has become the essence of the sublime since Romanticism, the same sensations
that Rilke and Yeats conjure through images of fearsome angels and a vi-
olating swan. Yet Ashbery creates sublime descent and recovery through
images of the mundane, those things that are always with us, like night
and day, like the persistence of lint, dust, and debris, those very things that
we most fear becoming. Yet in the face of oblivion, the potential to "surge
upward," "bursting into bloom," emerges from the terror and survival of
grade school, of uncertainty and defeat, of night and day.

Harold Bloom, one of the poet's earliest and most enthusiastic cham-
pions, reads the poems from this middle period of Ashbery's career as an
example of what he calls "the indisputable American Sublime," and he
links the work to Emerson in particular, citing this passage: "This insight,
which expresses itself by what is called Imagination, is a very high sort of
seeing, which does not come by study, but by the intellect being where and
what it sees; by sharing the path or circuit of things through forms and so
making them translucid to others."[8] The phrase "the intellect being where
and what it sees" feels especially apt for considering the poems of *The Double Dream of Spring*, and the second poem in the book, "Spring Day," illustrates the centrality of mind entering the outer space of objects in the
external environment, simultaneously raising the question of whether
mind should be thought of as a singular or multiple presence, enclosed
within a self or dispersed into the environment:

In so many phases the head slips from the hand.
The tears ride freely, laughs or sobs:

---

[7] Ashbery, "Sortes Vergilianae," in *The Double Dream of Spring*, 75.

[8] Harold Bloom, *Agon: Toward a Theory of Revisionism* (Oxford: Oxford
University Press, 1982), 276.

What do they matter? There is free giving and taking;
The giant body relaxed as though beside a stream

Wakens to the force of it and has to recognize
The secret sweetness before it turns into life—
Sucked out of many exchanges, torn from the womb,
Disinterred before completely dead—and heaves

Its mountain-broad chest.[9]

The poem opens with "immense hope, and forbearance" for the new
day, and plays out a mock battle with clubs and knives against the doubts
and bad dreams of night. The occasion for the poem is simply waking up
to the day. The speaker captures some of the lonely pleasure of the aubade,
the morning poem, and "has to recognize / The secret sweetness before it
turns into life—." Then the poem takes an unexpected turn, introducing a
long quote from an unidentified second speaker, who in turn introduces a
group of others, also unnamed:

"...They were presumed dead,
Their names honorably grafted on the landscape

To be a memory to men. Until today
We have been living in their shell.
Now we break forth like a river breaking through a dam,
Pausing over the puzzled, frightened plain,

And our further progress shall be terrible,
Turning fresh knives in the wounds
In that gulf of recreation, that bare canvas
As matter-of-fact as the traffic and the day's noise."

The mountain stopped shaking; its body
Arched into its own contradiction, its enjoyment...[10]

---

[9] Ashbery, "Spring Day," in *The Double Dream of Spring*, 14.
[10] Ibid.

A reader may feel tempted to risk the heresy of paraphrase, as an earlier generation of critics called it, but what could be said about the narrative logic of the passage? The important development of the second speaker is the striking change of tone and the intensification the introduction of violence brings to the poem. In his essay, "Vision in the Form of a Task," from *Beyond Amazement: New Essays on John Ashbery*, Charles Berger claims that the two voices are not oppositional but rather blended to represent two components of one self, suggesting that the second voice is that of the giant mentioned by the first speaker, who "may be seen as the sleeping Albion within us all, ear attuned to the primordial desire for freedom and release, a river that speaks only at the first breaking of day, and then goes underground, like Arnold's buried stream."[11] The voice indicates the sublime desire of dreams, when only the self must be gratified, unbound by social obligation or decorum, when the chance to break free from the yoke of tradition, the "names honorably grafted," might be attainable despite the bloody consequences.

"Spring Day" articulates the sublime dislocation of having a second self outside, or perhaps buried deep within, the primary self, existing among the contradictions of desire and performance, and the last quarter of the poem delivers the full effects of the emerging day:

> Wha—what happened? You are with
> The orange tree, so that its summer produce
> Can go back to where we got it wrong, then drip gently
> Into history, if it wants to. A page turned; we were
>
> Just now floundering in the wind of its colossal death.
> And whether it is Thursday, or the day is stormy,
> With thunder and rain, or the birds attack each other,
> We have rolled into another dream.
>
> No use charging the barriers of that other:
> It no longer exists. But you,

---

[11] Charles Berger, "Vision in the Form of a Task," in *Beyond Amazement: New Essays on John Ashbery*, ed. David Lehman (Ithaca: Cornell University Press, 1980), 169.

Gracious and growing thing, with those leaves like stars,
We shall soon give all our attention to you.[12]

The rising of the sun is greeted with a disgruntled and half-asleep question, "Wha—what happened?" and the unwelcome new day opens to roll "into another dream," that of waking life. The recompense that follows the sublime action of the giant's speech flounders at first in the indifference of the ordinary day, spent not in pursuit of the dream but in turning all attention to the merely beautiful objects and people of the world, the orange tree, the gracious and growing thing. The speaker, however, accepts this new responsibility not with disappointment but with generosity and love, prompting Berger's observation that the speakers' attitude "is a deeply moving emblem upon which to end a poem: we are entreated to care for the earth's own sublimity."[13]

Any study of the natural sublime in post-Romantic poetry must take the influence of Wordsworth fully into account. Ashbery is often aligned with Wordsworthian poetics because both developed poetries of interior spaces, in which the poet's observations and realizations—the growth of the poet's mind, so to speak—are the major sources of inspiration as well as revelation. Though more than one critic has called Ashbery the last great Romantic poet, Charles Altieri has countered this suggestion by claiming,

> ...like all the poets who recognize the need to transform lyric modes in order to save them from their own indulgences, Ashbery struggles to find an attitude by which one earns and explores a self-conscious rhetoric in reaction against rhetorics that claim naturalness. In this respect, at least, romanticism must die. There is no dream of a purified language. In fact, impurity of language becomes a mark of authenticity, since it registers the poet's awareness of the duplicity of discourse and the complexity of intentions. Impurity is our freedom and our salvation.[14]

For Wordsworth, the goal was to know the world through the self, and the world reciprocated by offering back to the self a playground for

---

[12] Ashbery, "Spring Day," 15.

[13] Berger, "Vision in the Form," 173.

[14] Charles Altieri, *Self and Sensibility in Contemporary American Poetry* (Cambridge: Cambridge University Press, 1984), 132.

the Imagination, a place where its limits and bounds could be explored and tested, a place where the self came to know itself. In Ashbery, as we have seen in "Spring Day," self-knowledge is a labyrinth of convexity and concavity, wherein the self may be surprised to run into alternate versions of its own being but also, as a recompense and consolation, can facilitate a dialogue between those various manifestations that generates a more comprehensive vision of an individual life. Altieri perceptively locates in Ashbery the recognition of "the poverty of representational means still uncontaminated by the spirit's sublimely destructive enterprise of attempting to know itself."[15] While certain limits of representational art have been visible in every age, it is a mistake to interpret Ashbery as a purely non-mimetic, non-conversational expressionist who deals primarily in abstractions, because he refuses to rend meaning entirely from image. Ashbery does not intend to show us a rocket ship when he writes "tree," or the victim of a global economic superstructure, and neither does "tree" show us a human heart. His images are not random or uncalculated, but they do successfully resist cliché and stock symbolic reference. While Altieri's argument does seem to negate the formulation of an egotistical sublime, as readers from Keats onward have termed the quality in Wordsworth's sense of self, this does not preclude the role of nature as a means of inspiration, as a model for determining the structure of meaning, or, in Ashbery's case, as the incoherent suggestion of meaning and form.

One could only pursue a partial discussion of the sublime in *The Double Dream of Spring* without examining the strong pull against the recompense and renewal that coexists beside such poems as "Summer," "Spring Day," "Evening in the Country," and "For John Clare." The book contains two of Ashbery's wildest and most successful parodies, "Variations, Calypso and Fugue on a Theme by Ella Wheeler Wilcox" and "Farm Implements and Rutabagas in a Landscape," both of which are explicit critiques of the sentimentality and false transcendence found in a certain type of nature poem, as well as implicit critiques of a culture that has merged the high and the low, the sublime and the ridiculous. "Farm Implements and Rutabagas in a Landscape" introduces characters from the comic strip "Popeye" and runs them through a tragicomic scenario in which Popeye's power-mad father has exiled him from his apartment. A paternal jealousy plot that spoofs all Oedipal tragedy from Shakespeare back through the .

---

[15] Ibid., 135.

Greeks emerges with Olive Oyl at the center, and Ashbery mixes the character's dialogue with the language of overwrought drama:

> Olive came hurtling through the window; its geraniums scratched
> Her long thigh. "I have news!" she gasped. "Popeye, forced as you
>   Know to flee the country
> One musty gusty evening, by the schemes of his wizened, duplicate
>   Father, jealous of the apartment
> And all that it contains, myself and spinach
> In particular, heaves bolts of loving thunder
> At his own astonished becoming, rupturing the pleasant
>
> Arpeggio of our years. No more shall the pleasant
> Rays of the sun refresh your sense of growing old, nor the scratched
> Tree-trunks and mossy foliage, only immaculate darkness and
>   Thunder."[16]

The comic effects succeed in the poem because the reader is so attuned to the language of both cartoons and serious drama, and the mixing of the two creates an absurdist play of misrecognition and confused identities. Sophisticated readers will also recognize Popeye's moment of sublime dislocation, when he "heaves bolts of loving thunder / At his own astonished becoming, rupturing the pleasant / Arpeggio of our years." Popeye's comfortable stasis has been interrupted by an outside plot, and he must confront his own new-fallen state. This is the condition of Hamlet, of Milton's Satan, of Oedipus upon learning of his crimes against nature, and we are informed by the tragic fates each of those characters experienced, yet Popeye is largely absent from his own tragedy, appearing from his exile only through his "undecoded messages." The poem continues to unfold based on the classic pattern of Longinian sublimity, allowing Popeye and the other characters a recovery from their sublime disjunction, not back into their original state of comfort but into a new condition of understanding, illuminated by having experienced the terror of uprootedness:

----

[16] Ashbery, "Farm Implements and Rutabagas in a Landscape," in *The Double Dream of Spring*, 47–48.

But Olive was already out of earshot. Now the apartment
Succumbed to a strange new hush. "Actually it's quite pleasant
Here," thought the Sea Hag. If this is all we need fear from spinach
Then I don't mind so much."[17]

Then the shockingly effective conclusion:
> ...Minute at first, the thunder
Soon filled the apartment. It was domestic thunder,
The color of spinach. Popeye chuckled and scratched
His balls: it sure was pleasant to spend a day in the country.[18]

In "Vision in the Form of a Task," Berger makes a useful claim about the significance of the parodies, stating, "What these experimental poems do best is to exaggerate and hypostatize thematic concerns and prosodic patterns that exist everywhere in *The Double Dream of Spring*."[19] Berger points to the extraordinary calibration Ashbery achieves in the volume, noting that while literary traditions are mocked, so are the ambitions toward structures of meaning found in other poems within the book, and that each parody has an analogue of serious examination elsewhere in the volume.

When considering the parodic element in Ashbery's work, it is worth remembering that the collection takes its name from a Giorgio di Chirico painting called *The Double Dream of Spring*, a surrealist landscape painting that shows a canvas in the foreground with a geometric image, possibly an abstract landscape, beside a human figure seen from the rear, and a view in the background out a window or from a terrace. The viewer's actual engagement with landscape stands once removed, perhaps twice removed. As the central landscape is abstracted, the literal landscape is viewed from distance with the space between the viewer and the ground interrupted by another viewer and by the abstract painting: one has to look past a set of obstacles to see it and to be made doubly aware of the importance of perspective in viewing art or nature. Ashbery's poetry portrays landscape in much the same way, insisting that the reader recognize the many filters between a viewer and his subject, while suggesting that the image may be

---

[17] Ibid., 48.
[18] Ibid.
[19] Berger, "Vision in the Form," 190.

obstructed by any number of perspectives. The gleam of surfaces holds great appeal for Ashbery, and just as he moves freely between tonal registers and levels of diction, he also slips from the sublime into the beautiful, or lingers in the midpoint of the picturesque, with seamless facility. Landscape is just as open for figurative use as literal use, the same as any other image, and can represent a relation with a larger symbolic structure or merely stand as the picture of its own physical presence. If images of the natural world are not open for experimental interpretation, for being seen and felt in new ways, then they no longer sustain the weight of depiction.

Edmund Burke provides the first important Romantic-era reading of sublimity in his 1757 study, *A Philosophical Enquiry into the Origin of Our Ideas of the Sublime and the Beautiful*, a text that shows the disparity between the effects of beauty and its darker, more compelling counterpart, the sublime. For Burke, beautiful objects are small, smooth, delicate, ornate, submissive, and light in tone and color, whereas the sublime embodies darkness, vastness, and magnificence; approaches infinity; and, most importantly, produces terror. The natural world, of course, demonstrates all of these qualities, spanning the full range of beauty and sublimity, and many of its features, rivers and mountains—to borrow the title of Ashbery's third volume of poetry—for instance, only yield to categorization when placed in a defining context, unlike, say, chrysanthemums, which can be either beautiful or not, depending on the taste of the observer, but never sublime.

In her book, *Solitude and the Sublime*, Frances Ferguson sheds an interesting light on the individuality produced in objects once they are given their defining context, and she implicitly points to a crucial difference between the Romantic sublime and the postmodern sublime:

> Nature, working on a vast scale, is adept at the striking particulars that design singles out, but no good at all on composition if we understand that process as one of organizing particulars within harmonious relationships.
>
> Composition, then, involves supplying a middle distance. And if the sublime aesthetic continually produces scenes in which the limitations of individual perception become tributes to the ability of human reason to think past those very perceptions, Gilpin's picturesque uses composition as a more routine way of insisting upon the centrality of the individual viewer. Mediating between nature's

vastness and the particulars of nature's design, the picturesque traveler searches for composable scenes.[20]

This distinction figures in an intriguing way in Ashbery's poems, because nature always works on a vast scale, though the particulars, which
are so central to the composition process, interest Ashbery less than the
enormity of the generality of nature. Even the title of his first collection of
poems, *Some Trees*, indicates the significance of imprecision in Ashbery's
vision. Unlike Gilpin's picturesque traveler, Ashbery finds the mediation
"between nature's vastness and the particulars of nature's design" perfectly
un-composable, and the emphasis on particular objects as building blocks
of a self-identity only creates a more unstable self. The lack of specificity
in Don DeLillo's 1985 novel *White Noise* offers a useful postmodern analogue: the characters live in an unspecified Midwestern city; their vocabu-
laries are infiltrated with a type of over-generalized government-speak,
with the "air-borne toxic event" and anagrams like SIMUVAC. They buy
groceries with plain white labels, named only by the contents of the pack-
age. DeLillo's villain, the deliberately named Mr. Gray, appears throughout the end of the novel as a staticky, out-of-focus amalgam, and even after
he physically appears, his talk is incoherent and he is seen only in the flick-
ering light of a hotel room television set. For DeLillo's characters in *White
Noise*, the vagueness creates a sense of dread, the nuclear sublime, as it is
for the speaker in Ashbery's "Definition of Blue," who says, "There is no
remedy for this 'packaging' which has supplanted the old sensations."[21]

The sublime in Ashbery's poetry often begins in dread or anxiety,
with a taking in of the vastness of surroundings, but his poetry is rich
enough to contain a wide range of sensations. Burke's emphasis on *delight*
as the key component of the sublime makes his thinking an interesting
backdrop for reading Ashbery, though where Burke pairs *delight* with *ambition*, Ashbery links *delight* with *ambivalence*. For Burke, delight appears
when terror subsides, after one is clear of the danger of personal harm. In
Ashbery's poems, delight works in a similar way, though without ever at-
taining the certainty of being free of danger, often because the danger itself

---

[20] Frances Ferguson, *Solitude and the Sublime: Romanticism and the Aesthetics
of Individuation* (New York: Routledge, 1992), 138. George H. Gilpin is a Hudson River School artist.

[21] Ashbery, "Definition of Blue," in *The Double Dream of Spring*, 53.

is a feeling, some component of the poem's atmosphere. If ambition signals desire—in the case of sublime recovery, a desire to know a threat has passed—and verifiable knowledge remains largely unattainable in Ashbery's poetry, then one must accept a delight rooted in an inevitable state of not-knowing. This ambivalence in Ashbery's work formulates the basis of what Bloom struggles to define as "a kind of Counter-Sublime that accepts a reduction of Whitmanian ecstasy while affirming it nevertheless…when the poet's whole soul is stirred into activity."[22] The reduction of Whitman is equally a reduction of Burke, though is it far from a dismissal—Ashbery finds a great deal of satisfaction in experience, even though language is untrustworthy and perceptions are free to shift based on perspective.

David LeHardy Sweet, in *Savage Sight/Constructed Noise*, his book on the modern French avant-garde, links Ashbery more closely with Mallarme and the French Symbolist poets (a movement Bloom dismisses as nonsense) than with Whitman and Stevens, the giants of the American sublime. Sweet says:

> The problem is that the "rottedness" Bloom identifies in Ashbery's poetry is less a matter of high and low speech than of language's own impediments to pure communication, to sheer transparency— a transparency Bloom likes to think of as the hallmark of the American sublime. Rather than seeing the fetidity of the words—their way of spoiling even in the process of communicating—as something to be suffered for redemptive purposes, French poets writing in the Symbolist tradition saw the virtue of allowing the language to "stink" a bit, to call attention to itself as a medium, to distract the reader from the domineering assumption of meaning.[23]

Sweet goes on to argue that this "putrefaction" is at the core of all early twentieth century avant-garde art movements, from cubism to surrealism, and sets a template for postmodern experimentation. Sweet's argument applies especially well to Ashbery's earliest two collections, to the mature strain in his work that includes "Farm Implements and Rutabagas

---

[22] Harold Bloom, *Figures of Capable Imagination* (New York: Seabury Press, 1976), 181.

[23] David LeHardy Sweet, *Savage Sight/Constructed Noise* (Chapel Hill: UNC Press, 2003), 243.

in a Landscape" and "Daffy Duck in Hollywood," and to the great parodies and jokes that include the one-line poems in *As We Know*, such as "We Were on the Terrace Drinking Gin and Tonics," the entirety of which reads, "when the squall hit."[24] Sweet's reading is overdetermined, however, when held up to certain of Ashbery's masterful long poems, such as "Fragment" from *The Double Dream of Spring* or "Self-Portrait in a Convex Mirror." Those poems, with their astonishing range and comprehensive study of a mind seriously engaged, as well their sweeping musicality, break through the constraining artifices of Symbolist methodology into something more expansive, an unbounded examination of the largely dejected human experience, with its essential dislocation from the self and its environment—something Burke might consider under the rubric of vastness.

Among the most accomplished of Ashbery's shorter lyric poems, "Soonest Mended" is also among his most autobiographical, what he calls his "'One-size-fits all confessional poem' which is about my youth and maturing but also about anybody else's."[25] The poem sets out to define an order for the self, a community into which the self may be situated, and finds only the fringes:

> Barely tolerated, living on the margin
> In our technological society, we were always having to be rescued
> On the brink of destruction, like heroines in *Orlando Furioso*
> Before it was time to start all over again.[26]

The echo of the title comes from the adage "Least said, soonest mended," and it describes the state the speaker hopes to find: "to be small and clear and free." But no one can hope to go unnoticed forever, and the speaker and his small band of outsiders suffer a moment of sublime dislocation:

> Only by that time we were in another chapter and confused
> About how to receive this latest piece of information.
> *Was* it information? Weren't we rather acting this out

---

[24] Ashbery, "We Were on the Terrace Drinking Gin and Tonics," in *As We Know: Poems* (New York: Viking, 1979), 74.

[25] Ashbery quoted in John Shoptaw, *On the Outside Looking Out: John Ashbery's Poetry* (Cambridge, MA: Harvard University Press, 1994), 105.

[26] Ashbery, "Soonest Mended," in *The Double Dream of Spring*, 17.

For someone else's benefit, thoughts in a mind
With room enough to spare for our little problems (so they began
    to seem),
Our daily quandary about food and the rent and bills to be paid?
To reduce all of this to a small variant,
To step free at last, miniscule on a gigantic plateau—
This was our ambition: to be small and clear and free.
Alas, the summer's energy wanes quickly.
A moment and it is gone. And no longer
May we make the necessary arrangements, simple as they are.
Our star was brighter perhaps when it had water in it.[27]

Thomas Gardner identifies the plateau, the moment of sublime recognition, as "what is not languageable—consciousness, the world outside of us, an other."[28] This is another way of portraying consciousness as landscape, seen clearly in Costello's suggestion that knowledge is understood through the metaphoric association with landscape. The speaker's exposure to the vastness of the world disorients him (or them, as the pronoun suggests), one who wants only freedom and finds overwhelming obligations and disappointments, and finds that the recompense is "learning to accept / The charity of the hard moments as they are doled out."

Peter de Bolla establishes the role of sublimity in the eighteenth century, which provides a useful view of the speaking/observing persona in Ashbery's poetry: "In this way the discourse of the sublime can be seen as one of the discourses present to the network which defines and enables the subject at a particular moment during the 18th century, and when seen from a particular perspective."[29] In Ashbery's poetry, specificity of place never generates the authority of perspective it carries in A. R. Ammons's "Corsons Inlet" or Gary Snyder's "Cold Mountain" and "Turtle Island," though his poems certainly carry a sense of engagement with place in a more general sense. The natural sublime, the occurrence of vastness and terror on the "giant plateau," gives the speaker in "Soonest Mended" a sense of place and dimension, wherein once more the landscape enables

---

[27] Ibid.

[28] Thomas Gardner, *Regions of Unlikeness: Explaining Contemporary Poetry* (Lincoln: University of Nebraska Press, 1999), 81.

[29] Peter de Bolla, *The Discourse of the Sublime: Readings in History, Aesthetics, and the Subject* (Oxford: Basil Blackwell, 1989), 17.

the speaker in an Ashbery poem to gauge his own existence. In keeping with the theme of Romantic consciousness, it is clear that poetry is the "lamp" in the natural world, even when utterly overwhelmed by its representation, and never simply the "mirror." The landscape enables, but it does not embody the speaker.

An impulse arises to link this sensibility with Wordsworth's version of the natural sublime, but what for Wordsworth was personal is for Ashbery impersonal. Mary Kinzie, however, counters any prospect of the egotistical sublime when she says of Ashbery, "He writes poems of detachment from affective experience without clinging to the elegiac experience of detaching himself."[30] Kinzie illustrates her point with a passage from "To John Clare," a prose poem from *The Double Dream of Spring*:

> It is possible that finally, like coming to the end of a long, barely perceptible rise, there is mutual cohesion and interaction....I say this because there is an uneasiness in things just now. Waiting for something to be over before you are forced to notice it. The pollarded trees scarcely bucking the wind—and yet it's keen, it makes you fall over....Meanwhile the whole history of probabilities is coming to life, starting in the upper left-hand corner, like a sail.[31]

Here again, anxiety in the speaker manifests in the landscape, with the trees barely fighting against the wind, and the metaphor for the point of disjunction, "the end of a barely perceptible rise," echoes the natural sublimity of the plateau in "Soonest Mended." Kinzie locates in "For John Clare" an "inevitability of non-entity"[32] and echoes John Koethe's position that Ashbery is everywhere struggling with the impulse to sublimity; however, because there is no "noble presence," no elevation into which one could transcend, the speaker responds to the perpetual unavailability of the Kantian sublime. While the poems are generally detached from affective experience, they are not detached from a sense of being in place.

The poetry of John Clare, a contemporary of Keats whose poems rely more on observations of village life than of mountain peaks, represents for Ashbery the authenticity of a poet living at one with his environment.

---

[30] Mary Kinzie, *The Cure of Poetry in an Age of Prose: Moral Essays on the Poet's Calling* (Chicago: University of Chicago Press, 1993), 260–61.

[31] Ashbery, "To John Clare," in *The Double Dream of Spring*, 254.

[32] Kinzie, *The Cure of Poetry*, 255.

Clare's observations of the minutiae of his native surroundings lead Ashbery to praise "his inspired *bricolage*" in the opening essay from his critical study, *Other Traditions*, based on his Charles Eliot Norton poetry lectures at Harvard University:

> Though the effect of Clare's poetry, on me at least, is always the same—that of re-inserting me in my present, of re-establishing "now"—the means he employs are endlessly varied despite the general air of artlessness. "The Village Minstrel," for instance, has a narrative glamour that is festive; the neatly turned epithets and sharp glimpses of village life fit together like an elaborate piece of clockwork as the tale of Lubin the minstrel unfolds. Clare stays very close to depicting the scene at hand until the end, when the village breaks open into a breathtaking panorama.[33]

Ashbery goes on to quote a long passage from "The Village Minstrel," in which the minstrel Lubin beholds his village as though looking down from a mountaintop, wishing that time would "explain her secrets" and let him know whether he will be embraced by the joy or the pain in his life. The lines beautifully construct the same sense of wonder and dread experienced by the speakers of such Ashbery poems as "Spring Day," "Soonest Mended," and "Evening in the Country."

In *Other Traditions*, Ashbery singles out in Clare's poetry the "great and enigmatic beauty" of the following passage from Clare's poem "The Elms and the Ashes," which he refers to as a personal talisman:

> The elm trees' heavy foliage meets the eye
> Propt in dark masses on the evening sky.
> The lighter ash but half obstructs the view,
> Leaving grey openings where the light looks through.

A similar moment of looking through "grey openings" occurs in Ashbery's own tribute, "For John Clare"; though in an urban scene, the observer experiences an "obstruction" of the view as well as a moment of incomprehension like that of the minstrel Lubin: "You are standing looking at that building and you cannot take it all in, certain details are already

---

[33] Ashbery, *Other Traditions* (Cambridge: Harvard University Press, 2001), 19.

hazy and the mind boggles."[34] In his book, *Walks in the World*, Roger Gilbert points out that "a consensus seems to have formed among most readers that Ashbery's poetry is entirely self-referential, to be admired or censured as such. Yet Ashbery himself, in statements and interviews, has consistently emphasized the mimetic function of his work, its effort to transcribe the experience of consciousness itself at its most elusive."[35] Indeed, Ashbery praises Clare for his very ability to represent what he has seen around him—the mimetic availability of the world to the poet—to which he responds with a consistently open and engaged mind, and displays his findings through a variety of poetic forms.

John Ashbery's poetry shifts modes of expression with great facility and can move from sublimity to the counter-sublime so deftly that one hardly notices that the register has changed. Throughout his long and highly prolific career, Ashbery's poetry has moved through many phases and modes, with succeeding volumes often hardly resembling one another. *The Double Dream of Spring* remains John Ashbery's most nature-infused collection of poems, and the one most immersed in the sublime, though he has not written since without some measure of the element of dislocation and recovery he developed in that book. Two of his most recent volumes, *Where Shall I Wander* (2005) and *A Worldly Country* (2007), return to the sensibility perhaps more than any of his intervening books. A central component of Ashbery's accomplishment lies in how successfully he abstracts the concrete, renders the everyday in unexpected ways, and makes the familiar strange. The most common details of landscape often rise up from their usual meanings to force a sublime disruption on an unsuspecting speaker, leaving the seeker of freedom and clarity "minuscule on the giant plateau." Because Ashbery works in opposition to traditional modes, the goal of mimesis in his poetry is not to show the world as it is, or to be reflected back to himself by a mirroring landscape, but rather to work through external interactions by means of an individual perspective and come to an understanding of those experiences that is true to the disjunction and incoherence found both in the self and in the world.

---

[34] Ashbery, "For John Clare," 35.

[35] Roger Gilbert, *Walks in the World: Representation and Experience in Modern American Poetry* (Princeton: Princeton University Press, 1991), 234.

PART 4

11

First Encounter:
James Agee's "Knoxville: Summer, 1915"

Childhood is full of secrets, mysteries, and disguises. I grew up in a remote, essentially eerie place way out in the country, with no neighbors or lights from other houses in sight. The evenings were quiet, and my mother and I often sat on the front porch and listened for bobwhites and whippoor-wills in the summer. If my father was home from work, he would join us, or my uncle Gerald, or my brother or sister, both half a generation older than me, and soon with children of their own. There was so much I did not understand, about the adults in my family, about the fears I experi-enced when I was too far in the woods by myself, about noises and shadows and changes in the atmosphere. I sensed that I was surrounded by myster-ies of every kind. I had all this uncertainty even though I lived with kind and loving people, a family that cared for me and gave me little reason for worry. The first time I read James Agee's brief poem-essay, "Knoxville: Summer, 1915," I felt I had seen through a window back into my own boyhood. The essay opens with an unforgettable *in medias res* sentence: *"We are talking now of summer evenings in Knoxville, Tennessee, in the time I lived there so successfully disguised to myself as a child."* That description caught me with such force, such immediacy, that it might as well have picked up in the middle of my own life.

The house I was raised in, and where my mother still lives today, was built in 1915. The house was less than forty miles from Knoxville, Tennessee, in the tiny Union County community of Sharps Chapel. Not only did Agee's place hold a deep personal resonance for me, but so did the date of his essay. I first read "Knoxville: Summer, 1915" as a first-year college student at Lincoln Memorial University, when my English professor, David Worley, advised me to read the writers who came from my part of the world. He mentioned Agee in particular, along with Thomas Wolfe and Wilma Dykeman. I knew a good deal of my own family history and a bit of the history of East Tennessee, but I did not know much about the rich literary background of Appalachia. I did not realize at the time that I was in the perfect setting to learn about it: the academic homeplace of George Scarbrough, Jesse Stuart, James Still, and Don West. When I read Agee, I could not believe that something so beautiful had been written about my part of the world, about a place I knew so well, and the people who lived there:

> *"They are not talking much, and the talk is quiet, of nothing in particular, of nothing at all in particular, of nothing at all. The stars are wide and alive, they seem each like a smile of great sweetness, and they seem very near. All my people are larger bodies than mine, quiet, with voices gentle and meaningless like the voices of sleeping birds."*

Most readers would have first encountered "Knoxville: Summer, 1915" as a kind of prologue to Agee's 1957 novel, *A Death in the Family*, published two years after Agee's premature death and the posthumous winner of the 1958 Pulitzer Prize for Fiction, though it was initially published in *The Partisan Review* in 1938. It seems Agee never intended for the essay to become part of his autobiographical novel, but his friend and literary executor, David McDowell, saw the powerful link between it and Agee's not-quite-finished fictional account of his childhood. Nearly a quarter of the piece—what even to call it…personal essay? prose poem? short story? meditation?—is devoted to describing the full-sensorial image of water leaving a hose and spraying across suburban lawns, and to depicting the sounds made by locusts. The writing may defy categorization by genre, but the trust and vulnerability of the child, and the serenity of his surroundings, creates an undeniably powerful emotional effect.

James Agee is considered one of the inventors of modern film criticism, and at least a couple of the films for which he wrote screenplays, certainly *The African Queen* and *Night of the Hunter*, are now considered classics. Some readers have proposed that Agee was poorly served by his versatility and that, had he written a half-dozen novels instead of the scattershot of various modes and styles, he would be much better known today. Samuel Barber retained a slightly altered version Agee's title and set the final part of the poem-essay to music, and that composition is surely more famous than Agee's original text. Yet "Knoxville: Summer, 1915" is as perfectly made as John Keats's "To Autumn," another great lyrical meditation on seasons and the passing of time. In the way that "To Autumn" distills the eternal essence of an entire season, repeated endlessly with small variations, Agee draws in all of childhood in "Knoxville: Summer, 1915." Agee parts a veil to reveal the grown-up each of us was always waiting to become, hidden inside the child we each for a brief time were.

More than a century has passed since the scene Agee described, and I feel just as moved, and bewildered, by his ability to evoke the mystery of childhood. Agee leaves me with the feeling that the world around any one person is vast, and while we can see much of what surrounds us, far more remains hidden. The closing words of "Knoxville: Summer, 1915" are perhaps the most profound I have ever read about a child's role in a family, and they sing in the incantatory way of distant memories:

> *"May god bless my people, my uncle, my aunt, my mother, my good father, oh, remember them kindly in their time of trouble; and in the hour of their taking away. After a little I am taken in and put to bed. Sleep, soft smiling, draws me unto her: and those receive me, who quietly treat me, as one familiar and well-beloved in that home: but will not, oh, will not, not now, not ever; but will not ever tell me who I am."*

12

A Blind Work of Nature:
The Ethics of Representing Beauty in
Let Us Now Praise Famous Men

Almost midway through his remarkable book, *Let Us Now Praise Famous Men*, in a brief and tormented consideration of intention in art, James Agee extends a philosophical question: "Are things beautiful which are not intended as such, but which are created as in convergences of chance, need, innocence or ignorance, or entirely irrelevant purposes?"[1] The question encompasses the very nature of Agee's project in Alabama and is intended to quantify his response to the house of George and Annie Mae Gudger, one of three tenant farming families whose lives are examined in his work with photographer Walker Evans. Many studies of *Let Us Now Praise Famous Men* have considered the importance of Agee's ethics and have separately examined his aesthetic principles, but none have looked closely at the critical consequence of aesthetic beauty in the formulation of Agee's ethical intentions for the book.[2] Though attempts to understand the role aesthetic

---

[1] James Agee and Walker Evans, *Let Us Now Praise Famous Men* (1941; Boston: Houghton-Mifflin, 2001), 178.

[2] Many of the earliest full-length studies on Agee, such as Mark A. Doty's *Tell Me Who I Am* (Baton Rouge: Louisiana State University Press, 1981) and Kenneth Seib's *James Agee: Promise and Fulfillment* (Pittsburgh: University of Pittsburgh Press, 1968), examine the ethics of *Let Us Now Praise Famous Men* but

beauty plays in both private and social actions go back at least to Plato's *Phaedrus*, much contemporary criticism has dismissed the search for beauty in favor of more seemingly tangible goals, such as political, sociological, and psychological motives and interpretations. Agee's interest in finding the unrecognized beauty in life, particularly in lives that are hidden from general view, drives much of what he sets out to accomplish in *Let Us Now Praise Famous Men*.

In the book's prologue, Agee admits to some confusion about his aims, but one thing that consistently emerges is his commitment to showing the actual living conditions of the tenant farmers. He shows particular attention to dwellings, and his most intense deliberations about aesthetics occur when examining such basic necessities as what the farmers eat and how they keep their houses. Agee sees two forms of "classicism" in the tenant houses, which are "beautifully euphonious" in their bringing together of need, availability, and "local-primitive traditions," though he acknowledges that they "are built in the 'stinginess,' carelessness, and traditions of an impersonal agency."[3] In other words, the particular type of beauty that he recognizes in the setting exists only to the eyes of a highly cultivated outside observer. Such a vision offers an essential element to the deep paradox of the undertaking of *Let Us Now Praise Famous Men*: how is this "sovereign prince of the English language"[4] to create a true docu-

---

do not explore their relationship to the book's position on artistic beauty. Victor A. Kramer, in *Agee and Actuality: Artistic Vision in His Work* (Troy, NY: Whitston, 1991), and James Lowe, in *The Creative Process of James Agee* (Baton Rouge: Louisiana State University Press, 1994), both consider Agee's aesthetics but are primarily concerned with his literary technique and how Agee created an image of the farm workers' way of life, not with the ethical outcomes of his representation of beauty. Recent works on Agee, such as Jeffrey J. Folks's "Agee's Angelic Ethics," in *Agee Agonistes: Essays on the Life, Legend, and Works of James Agee*, ed. Michael A. Lofaro (Knoxville: University of Tennessee Press, 2007), and Hugh Davis's *The Making of James Agee* (Knoxville: University of Tennessee Press, 2008) take compelling looks at specific aspects of Agee's ethics and aesthetics, such as the influence of Gnostic theology or European surrealism.

[3] Agee and Evans, *Famous Men*, 178.

[4] Agee was given this title by Robert Phelps in his prefatory essay to James Agee, *The Letters of James Agee to Father Flye* (New York: George Braziller, 1962),

ment about the lives of individuals toward whom he feels a deeply personal, almost familial bond without exploiting the beauty he finds in them, which they themselves are not schooled to recognize? The only way through this paradox, and into the real meaning of the book, involves interpreting Agee both at and against his word about the use and function of art, and as corrupted as Agee may contend that it is, art ranks high on his list of debased "anglosaxon monosyllables."[5] The expression of human feeling through beauty provides the only means by which a family such as the Gudgers can hope to receive any form of recognition in the world and, consequently, any form of justice.

One of the chief complaints against *Let Us Now Praise Famous Men* upon its release in 1941 was the chronic imposition of Agee's own wandering, occasionally vulgar self-consciousness into the book, which was supposed to explore the sufferings of the most deeply underprivileged members of our society.[6] If Agee had promised a work of pure documentary exposition, then such criticisms would not have been unwarranted. The ethics of this book, however, and of Agee's lifelong aesthetic mission, required not only that the tenant families are shown but also that they are understood, that their lives are given a fully integrated place in the world, even if that involved linking them to meanings and precedents they might have neither recognized nor understood. These are the ethics that permit Agee to make one of his greatest leaps of continuation and symbiosis, which also tips his hand toward his honest vision of art (as it opposes

---

1. James Harold Flye, the "Father Flye" of Agee's celebrated letters, is also quoted in Ross Spears's documentary film about Agee's life using the same "title" (*Agee,* dir. Ross Spears, James Agee Film Project, 1980). Flye was a teacher of Agee's at St. Andrew's School in Sewanee, Tennessee, and remained a friend until the end of Agee's life.

[5] Agee and Evans, *Famous Men,* 403.

[6] A representative example of this complaint is L. R. Etzkorn's review (*Library Journal* 66 [Aug 1941]: 667), in which he claims that the "author has included a mass of unrelated, nonsensical material, some parts almost the ravings of a lunatic, while others are beautiful, lyric prose of high merit, not entirely related to sharecropping." Other examples would include George Barker's review "Three Tenant Families" (*Nation,* Sept 27, 1941, 282) and Selden Rodman's review "The Poetry of Poverty" in *Saturday Review* (Aug 23, 1941, 6).

"Art") when he reconfigures his answer to the original question about artistic intention: "Or: the Beethoven piano concerto #4 IS importantly, among other things, a 'blind' work of 'nature,' of the world and of the human race; and the partition wall of the Gudgers' front bedroom IS importantly, among other things, a great tragic poem."[7] An examination of the intersection between private and social ethics with aesthetic interpretation demonstrates that, for Agee, the ethical and the beautiful cannot be separated through either intention or accident.

A thought closely attuned to the problems of Agee's uncertainties is used by Elaine Scarry to close the first section of her meditation on the ethics of recognizing beauty, *On Beauty and Being Just*. In her chapter "On Beauty and Being Wrong," she claims that beauty and truth are allied but not identical conditions, stating,

> It is not that a poem or a painting or a palm tree or a person is "true," but rather that it ignites the desire for truth by giving us, with an electric brightness shared by almost no other uninvited, freely arriving perceptual event, the experience of conviction and the experience, as well, of error.[8]

Beauty can lead one to act rashly or quickly, without clarity of vision or purpose, in ways that may in fact run counter to the good of the admired object. Scarry's observation appears more than sixty years after Agee confronts the likenesses and terrible separations between the bedroom décor of an impoverished country family and a Beethoven concerto that represents a pinnacle of Western artistic accomplishment, yet her conclusion falls very much in line with Agee's fears about the impossibility of representing with any accuracy the beauty of the lives he observes in Alabama. The error Agee wishes to avoid involves turning the families into representative examples of tenant farmers, objectifying their experiences as members of an unfortunate group, which, incidentally, is exactly what the *Fortune* magazine assignment prompted him to do. For Agee, however, the Gudgers, Ricketts, and Woods are not objects but individuals.

A difficult balance between conviction and error is introduced early

---

[7] Agee and Evans, *Famous Men*, 179.

[8] Elaine Scarry, *On Beauty and Being Just* (Princeton: Princeton University Press, 1999), 52.

in *Let Us Now Praise Famous Men*, as witnessed in the often-quoted statement from the introductory section, which bears considering again here in this particular context, in which Agee announces that, "If I could do it, I'd do no writing at all here. It would be photographs; the rest would be fragments of cloth, bits of cotton, lumps of earth, records of speech, pieces of wood and iron, phials of odors, plates of food and of excrement."[9] Evan Carton and Janis Bergman-Carton suggest that Agee's desire in this famous passage "is not to render lived experience without linguistic mediation so much as it is to sacralize both language and experience on the altar of the Real—a ceremony requiring the recreation or replication of life and the living in the house of God or art."[10] It is worth noting that the evocations that make up the vast catalogues and inventories of large parts of the book attempt exactly this sort of beyond-cerebral effect and that Agee pushes his wish even further: "A piece of the body torn out by the roots might be more to the point."[11] Agee concedes that the immensely flawed prospect of writing is all he can offer, given that it is the only developed tool with which he has to work. Agee's conviction to communicate the Gudgers' ways and means of life is undeniable, and so is his intuitive recognition of the potential for error. The consequences of making the kind of error that Scarry later describes nearly paralyze his efforts to substantiate the Gudgers' experience: Agee worked on the project for nearly five years before arriving at its final form.

Agee revisits the possibility for this type of well-intentioned error in the later section titled "On the Porch: 2," which critic William Stott calls "the book's intellectual center,"[12] by way of a telling footnote. Agee has

---

[9] Agee and Evans, *Famous Men*, 10.

[10] Evan Carton and Janis Bergman-Carton, "James Agee, Walker Evans: Tenants in the House of Art," *Raritan: A Quarterly Review* 20, no. 4 (Spring 2001): 3.

[11] Agee and Evans, *Famous Men*, 10.

[12] William Stott suggests that "'On the Porch: 2' may well contain some of Agee's most ideological writing, but also demonstrates a number of the book's abiding contradictions; namely that Agee dismisses journalism as 'a broad and successful form of lying' (207) and that he both advances the potential for language to 'be made to do or to tell anything within human conceit' (209) and discounts their actual value on the following: 'Words cannot embody; they can only describe' (210)" (William Stott, *Documentary Expression and Thirties America*

been discussing the demerits of literary "naturalism" as a means of expressing reality, suggesting instead that for documentation to have "any value equivalent" to fiction or poetry, it must not only be presented but also talked about, and that the way it is presented must also be discussed. The following phrase is so compelling that it requires quoting with addendum intact: "I feel sure in advance that any efforts, in what follows, along the lines I have been speaking of will be failures"; the footnote reads, "*Failure, indeed, is almost as strongly an obligation as an inevitability, in such work: and therein sits the deadliest trap of an exhausted conscience.*"[13] Elaine Scarry never goes so far as to say that error and failure are the same, unless of course one might consider the undertaking of a task failed a priori to be an error of judgment, if not of execution.

In an earlier work, titled *The Body in Pain,* Scarry introduces certain structures for examining the "inexpressibility of physical pain"[14] as well as the "political consequences" of that impossibility of clear expression or, to use a term more typical of Agee, "embodiment." *The Body in Pain* is a broad-ranging study that encompasses the spectrum of creative arts as well as law, medicine, and public policy, but *Let Us Now Praise Famous Men* also addresses each of these terrains, albeit with a less specified approach, because Agee is committed to engaging the whole life of his subjects, the full "importance and dignity and of actuality."[15] Scarry's claim in the "Introduction" to *The Body in Pain* sheds some light on why Agee feels compelled to bring the sharecroppers' lives into public scrutiny:

> When one hears about another person's physical pain, the events happening within the interior of that person's body may seem to have the remote character of some deep subterranean fact, belonging to an invisible geography that, however portentous, has no reality because it has not yet manifested itself on the visible surface of the earth.[16]

The task for Agee, and equally for Evans, then becomes finding a

---

[New York: Oxford University Press, 1973], 296).

[13] Agee and Evans, *Famous Men,* 210.

[14] Scarry, *The Body in Pain: The Making and Unmaking of the World* (New York: Oxford University Press, 1985) 3.

[15] Agee and Evans, *Famous Men,* 216.

[16] Scarry, *The Body in Pain,* 3.

means through which to engage the beauty and the dignity of the individual tenant farmer's life, while also indicting the system of economics and social injustice that displaces them from any of the comforts or securities that most members of the society enjoy, and to do so without sentimentalizing or romanticizing their lifestyle or character. Perhaps no phrase in the language better captures the expression of George Gudger in Walker Evans's famous portrait than the "deep subterranean fact" of Gudger's pain. This is the image that stares out from the cover of Houghton Mifflin's 2001 edition of *Let Us Now Praise Famous Men*, an apt representation of the book itself. In the instance of this and many other of the medium-range, direct-address portraits, the pain Evans evokes is not easily discernible as purely physical, because the photographs, like the prose text, suggest no one single aspect of living but the whole of it—the physical, the emotional, and the spiritual all condensed into one moment of expression. For the observer, the resonance of the images lies in knowing that in the world of their lived existence, the people these faces represent have no agency whatsoever in the world of politics, economics, or self-expression. One cannot read the aesthetics of the photographs, or of Agee's examination of the family sleeping arrangements, without recognizing that agency and again justice, such as it can be, are granted only through the creation and exhibition of the artworks these lives have generated and inspired.

Neither the text nor the photographs of *Let Us Now Praise Famous Men* allow the observer an uncomplicated perspective. In meaningful ways, the two forms as expressed seem not to go together; the photographs are too clearly focused and the cleanliness of the images clashes with the disorderliness of the text's structure, while the clutter of emotions and interpretations offered by Agee's hyper-sensitive prose appears out of step with the coolly detached temper of the pictures. Mark Durden provides an interesting reading of these aesthetic differences in a brief and informative essay on the book titled "The Limits of Modernism." Durden points out that "Evans remains much more distanced and disengaged than Agee,"[17]

---

[17] Durden goes further into the potential aesthetic reasons for this: "The photographer has a self-effacing view of photography, modeled on the modernist 'writing degree zero' of Flaubert. Evans desires to minimize subjectivity: 'Flaubert's aesthetic is absolutely mine: the non-appearance of the author, the non-subjectivity.' Yet while this modernist aesthetic accords with a classic of observational documentary—objective and matter of fact—Evans's disengagement with

indicating the tensions between Evans's minimal attachment and Agee's maximal immersion. The implication of such an analysis, quite correctly, is that there are two models of representing beauty at work in the book and that it is impossible to separate the ideals of each without distinguishing the two equally divergent approaches to the ethical circumstances of the project. For Evans, distance means clarity, impartiality, and authenticity, which is not to say that Evans cares less than Agee about the particular subjects or even that he cares more for the beauty of the images than for the suffering they represent. A fair assumption might be that Evans believes that the force of the unadulterated images will convey everything an observer needs to know to judge accurately the conditions of the tenant farmers' lives; the pictures will speak for themselves. Perhaps Agee's deepest belief in the entire book is that nothing separates the lives of the tenant farmers from his own life, and from the lives of his potential readers, so much as the division between economic classes. In Agee's case, the only distance that could exist between himself and the actual people about whom he writes is the artificial distance of social class (which comes with many real distancing devices, such as barely fathomable divides of educational opportunity and domestic comfort), and this artificial distance is not only an aesthetic liability[18] but also personally damaging and constitutes an immoral act.

Agee and Evans share an equal commitment to showing the subjects of their work as identifiable individuals, counter to the prevalent tendency of other documentary books of the 1930s, such as *You Have Seen Their Faces* by Erskine Caldwell and Margaret Bourke-White[19] and *An American Exodus* by Dorothea Lange and Paul Taylor.[20] Those books tend to show

---

his subjects is indirectly called into question by Agee as he struggles to get close to the tenant families" (26). Durden concludes, "As much as there are moments when Agee looks toward photography with envy in his text, ultimately his writing invokes the need for a photo-praxis that is more self-conscious than Evans's. Agee's reflexive, engaged, and impassioned writing alerts us to the limits of Evan's modernism" (29). See Mark Durden, "The Limits of Modernism," *Literary Modernism and Photography*, ed. Paul Hansom (Westport: Praeger, 2002).

[18] Agee values most highly those artists who refuse distance, who approach every subject as near to its burning core as possible: D. H. Lawrence, William Blake, James Joyce, Beethoven, and Van Gogh, among others.

[19] New York: Viking, 1937.

[20] New York: Reynal and Hitchcock, 1939.

the lives of the poor as part of a social or economic trend or to present people as representative samples from a larger (and by implication more significant) group experience. Evans achieves this goal of individual identification by allowing each person to prepare himself or herself for the photograph just as they would for a family portrait—thus they are seen as they would wish to be seen, and the unguarded results characterize the deep and lasting results of Evans's accomplishment. This allows Evans to create a contrast in both tone and temperament with the emotionally outsized and psychologically overdetermined pictures of Southern farmers taken by other documentary artists, such as Margaret Bourke-White. Art critic Margaret Olin raises a salient point about the impact of the photographic approach Evans chooses: "What is hard about gazing into someone's eyes is that oneself is seen as well."[21] Olin's statement bears implications for Agee's text as well, in one sense because *he* feels the gaze of his hosts so intently and in a further sense because in order to communicate their lives fully, he must make *us* feel their gaze as well. It corresponds with his central goal of making ignorance of the families' circumstances impossible to ignore and of embodying the divinity of even the most obscured life: "I am being made witness to matters no human being may see."[22]

Agee's acute attention to detail, to the implied significance of even the smallest instance, informs the rationale behind the considerable time spent in the book cataloguing the items belonging to the families, giving generally not merely a list of things seen but as careful and thorough a characterization of the things' qualities as his experience permits. The description of the food he is served when he returns to the Gudgers' house after his car stalls goes into the minutiae of taste and nuance: "The jam is loose, of little berries, full of light raspings of the tongue; it tastes a deep sweet purple tepidly watered, with a very faint sheen of sourness as of iron."[23] This is in one sense a passage of descriptive prose, employing certain poetic devices, such as the synesthetic assigning of a definite flavor to the abstract color purple and the creating of an analogic relationship with the taste of iron. In this instance, Agee makes an aesthetic choice: rather than describe in the clearest and most journalistic manner the food he has been served, he elects instead to represent that food with the figurative

---

[21] Margaret Olin, "It Is Not Going to Be Easy to Look into Their Eyes," *Art History* 14, no. 1 (1991): 97.

[22] Agee and Evans, *Famous Men*, 120.

[23] Ibid., 366.

language of poetry or prose fiction. Whether the aesthetic principle of such writing is appropriate to the nature of the particular book remains debatable, but it must also be acknowledged that style is an ethical choice as well, in which Agee chooses the individual over the generic, uniqueness over commonality. His extensive cataloguing of detail represents an effort at distinguishing the singular nature of each person he writes about, every trait or possession one component of the entire self and being of an individual like no other.

One of the most effective interpretations of Agee's catalogue approach comes from Jeanne Follansbee Quinn, who points to Agee's recognition of the difficulty with this level of specificity, noting that "identification was both an aesthetic and political problem: it was a phenomenological effect of language with social and political consequences."[24] Quinn considers Agee neither a liberal nor a Marxist, but rather a pragmatist[25] who understands the usefulness of irony as a tool for responding to oppression and as a component for defining an individual perspective. Agee states as much in the preface to *Let Us Now Praise Famous Men*, which he encourages "serious readers" to skip, by simultaneously setting the bar for his project impossibly high and relieving himself of any obligation beyond recognition, which he admits will be difficult enough:

> Actually the effort is to recognize the stature of a portion of unimagined existence, and to contrive techniques proper to its recording, communication, analysis, and defense. More essentially, this is an independent inquiry into certain normal predicaments of human divinity.
>
> The immediate instruments are two: the motionless camera, and the printed word. The governing instrument—which is also one of the centers of the subject—is individual, anti-authoritative

---

[24] Jeanne Follansbee Quinn, "The Work of Art: Irony and Identification in *Let Us Now Praise Famous Men*," *Novel: A Forum on Fiction* 34, no. 3 (1991): 338.

[25] John Hersey says of Agee, "His political consciousness was that of a revolutionary, but one who saw that all revolutionaries are fallible human beings, often wicked, cruel, power-mad." See John Hersey, "Introduction: Agee," in *Famous Men*, xxx.

human consciousness.[26]

One must acknowledge two facts about these paragraphs: first, that the earlier paragraph introduces not only a contract with the book's readers but also an ethical responsibility, and second, that the two "immediate instruments," and especially the "governing instrument," are the tools of art and that the "individual, anti-authoritative" document he intends to create is guided by this same aesthetic prescription.[27]

One senses what a cruel irony and an irreconcilable pain it causes Agee that the beauty he recognizes in the Gudgers' front bedroom cannot be appreciated by those who would benefit most from its presence, the Gudgers themselves. In an especially poignant moment, just after Agee has left off his discussion of beauty and the classical form of the bedroom's simple designs, he says:

> Since I have talked of "esthetics" the least I can do is to add a note on it in their terms: they live in a steady shame and insult of discomforts, insecurities, and inferiorities, piecing these together into whatever semblance of comfortable living they can, and the whole of it is a stark nakedness of makeshifts and the lack of means: yet they are also, of course, profoundly anesthetized. The only direct opinion I got on the houses as such was from Mrs. Gudger, and it was with tears coming to her eyes, "Oh, I do *hate* this house *so bad!* Seems like they ain't nothing in the whole world I can do to make it pretty."[28]

Even though Mrs. Gudger has only the poorest materials with which to decorate, she attempts to make the house as pretty as she is able. The results, for Agee as for John Keats in an earlier century, are beautiful because they are true, because they have the authenticity of a single, imperfect, human perspective.

---

[26] Agee and Evans, *Famous Men*, x.

[27] This amounts to what Alfred Kazin calls Agee's "revolt against the automatism of the documentary school." It is notable that Kazin also called *Let Us Now Praise Famous Men* "the documentary book to end all documentary books," the very book in which Agee criticizes Kazin for his unsympathetic reading of Louis-Ferdinand Celine (*Famous Men*, 11). See Alfred Kazin, *On Native Grounds: An Interpretation of Modern Prose Literature* (1942; San Diego: Harvest, 1995), 495.

[28] Agee and Evans, *Famous Men*, 184.

An early response to *Let Us Now Praise Famous Men* by esteemed literary critic Lionel Trilling provides an insightful context with which to conclude a cross-examination of ethics and aesthetics. The review, "Greatness with One Fault in It," is on the whole very favorable toward the book; indeed, Trilling calls it "the most realistic and important moral effort of our American generation."[29] It might seem overly particular, then, to take issue with the complaint that Trilling characterizes as the "one fault," but it is a matter of tremendous importance to the meaning of Agee's book:

> The failure I referred to is certainly not literary; it is a failure of moral realism. It lies in Agee's inability to see *these people* [italics added] as anything but good. Not that he falsifies what is apparent: for example he can note with perfect directness their hatred of Negroes; and not that he is ever pious or sentimental, like Steinbeck or Hemingway. But he writes of his people as if there were no human unregenerateness in them, no flicker of malice or meanness, no darkness or wildness of feeling, only a sure and simple virtue, the growth, we must suppose, of their hard, unlovely poverty.[30]

Trilling attributes this shortcoming to Agee's immense "guilt" about the comparative quality of his own life versus the lives of the sharecroppers about whom he writes. Trilling's misreading here involves not simply failing to understand the subjects of his critique, both Agee and the tenant farmers, but also an inability to recognize the element from which those subjects emerge. Agee does not show (for the most part) "meanness" or "malice" in the actions of the family members, but shows instead the myriad ways in which their whole existences are immersed in the conditions of meanness and malice.

Trilling emerges guilty perhaps, exactly as Agee anticipated his audience of cultural elites would be, of the very sort of moral judgment from whose subjection Agee excuses the tenant farmers. An underlying and implied question throughout the text is, how can any of the rest of us, the observers in our relative comfort and ease, begin to judge the moral or political or spiritual by-products of lives that are so grossly underserved by the wealth and well-being experienced within the greater society? The "human unregenerateness" of the sort that Trilling anticipates would

[29] Lionel Trilling, "Greatness with One Fault in It," *Kenyon Review* 4 (1942): 102.
[30] Trilling, "Greatness with One Fault," 102.

barely be called human at all if it were present in a different class of individuals, but it would be looked upon rather as an aberration, a willful desertion of one's cultural responsibility. Agee does not suggest that either goodness or the lack of malice is the outgrowth of poverty. "Human unregenerateness" is not a characteristic either present in or absent from a particular representation of the circumstances of a certain group of three Alabama tenant families; like the beauty that expresses itself as "a blind work of Nature" in the farmers' lives, unregenerateness is simply a primary quality of their lives.

The youthful Agee in *Let Us Now Praise Famous Men* is a paradoxical figure, a sentimentalist who despises sentimentality, an affirmer who rejects affirmation, and most grandly, a discounter of all that he so obviously values most highly—see again his list of "anglosaxon monosyllables." Agee finds an inherent beauty in the lives of the tenant farmers he observes, not a superficial or calculated form of beauty but a quality that grows in natural response to their lives. His book abounds in seeming contradictions, and he himself is unable to make a unified response to his age and the problems it presents any sensitive, impassioned young mind. But he does accomplish a significant feat in this document on the lives of the Alabama tenant farmers with whom he lived: he presents their lives with all the dignity and importance another writer might assign to the "great men" of any period, and he does so without compromising either his aesthetic vision or his ethical foundation. And ultimately Agee achieves a unified field of actual lives lived, with their often-troubling, endlessly persevering destinies made apparent.

13

Parallel Poetics:
Ways of Seeing in James Agee and
Federico García Lorca

James Agee and Federico García Lorca began their lives on separate continents and in very different social worlds, though only a decade separated their births. Agee was raised in Knoxville, Tennessee, in what he called "a little bit mixed sort of block, fairly solidly lower middle class, with one or two juts apiece on either side of that."[1] In 1899, Lorca was born in Spain, near the Andalusian city of Granada, into a family of wealth and privilege. Though the home lives of their childhoods were quite distinct, they lived through the same global events and took part in the same intellectual debates and conflicts. Less than a decade before James Agee and Walker Evans took their *Fortune* magazine assignment and headed to rural Alabama, Federico García Lorca left his native Andalusia region of Spain to spend the academic year of 1929–1930 at Columbia University in New York City. Given the considerable number and nature of differences between the two writers' lives, many striking intersections can be found in their works. Both writers began as poets and wrote always in a lyrical style

---

[1] James Agee, *A Death in the Family: A Restoration of the Author's Text*, ed. Michael A. Lofaro, vol. 1 of *The Works of James Agee*, ed. Michael A. Lofaro and Hugh Davis (Knoxville: University Press of Tennessee, 2010), 565. Quoted here from an appendix, "Knoxville: Summer of 1915" was published as a prologue to the novel in the 1957 McDowell version.

which revealed that background, while becoming better known later for working in other genres. Two books in particular reveal their shared sensibilities, Lorca's *Poet in New York*, begun in 1929 and published posthumously in various versions beginning in 1940, and Agee's *Let Us Now Praise Famous Men*, begun in 1936 and published in 1941. These two books share not just a random assortment of similarities but a fundamental likeness of endeavor, an aim to embody the spirit of a particular place through an unsentimental view of the ways of life of its inhabitants, taking a special focus on those who live with the greatest hardships and the least security.

James Agee's boyhood in East Tennessee may have prepared him, somewhat, for the poverty he found in Hale County, Alabama, when he arrived with Walker Evans to complete their magazine assignment. Agee makes his purpose for the book clear: "The nominal subject is North American cotton tenantry as examined in the daily living of three representative white tenant families."[2] He had seen country life firsthand, visiting his father's family in the rural counties north of the city of Knoxville. Agee could even modulate his accent to make himself sound like less of an outsider to the Alabama sharecroppers whose lives he was there to document. Nothing, however, had prepared Lorca for the urban poverty he would encounter in New York City in the fall of 1929. His upbringing had been near idyllic, growing up in an artistic and musical family who were not unlike Agee's relations on his mother's side. What Lorca found in New York shocked the young man, as witnessed in the poem "Dawn":

> Dawn in New York has
> Four columns of mire
> And a hurricane of black pigeons
> Splashing in the putrid waters[3]

Certain biographical similarities between the two writers provide an interesting groundwork for the ways in which their works run parallel.

---

[2] James Agee and Walker Evans, *Let Us Now Praise Famous Men: An Annotated Edition of the James Agee–Walker Evans Classic, with Supplementary Manuscripts*, ed. Hugh Davis, vol. 3 of *The Works of James Agee*, ed. Michael A. Lofaro and Hugh Davis (Knoxville: University of Tennessee Press, 2014), x.

[3] Federico García Lorca, *Poet in New York*, ed. Christopher Maurer (New York: Farrar, Straus, and Giroux, 1998), 73, ll. 1–4.

Agee and Lorca were raised in the early part of the twentieth century, in regions of their respective countries known for political conservatism—particularly concerning matters of race and class—and for especially devout religious communities. Beyond the similarities of the two authors' personal circumstances, the two texts also share some elements of a common fate. Both books suffered considerable delay before publication, though for very different reasons. The well-documented stories of how the books finally reached the audiences that eventually would declare them masterpieces must certainly contribute to the near-mythical status of their authors.

Both writers looked closely at their own childhood experiences in earlier works and used autobiographical materials freely. A number of common tonalities and images exist between Agee's "Knoxville: Summer of 1915" and Lorca's "Ballad of the Three Rivers" and "Landscape," from his 1921 collection *Poem of the Deep Song*. Agee gives as lyrical a depiction of suburban America as one is likely to find, with many details about food, work, trees, and how people spent their time together. For Lorca, the "Deep Song," or "*Cante Jondo*," was the last true expression of Spanish folk-life. As in most instances, Lorca's descriptions in these poems are more elliptical than Agee's—"The river Guadalquivir / Has garnet whiskers,"[4] for example—but still firmly rooted in the traditions of his place. The subject matter and contents of both books emerge out of other materials, or other intentions. Neither Agee nor Lorca set out to write these particular texts. Agee initially was writing for a specific assignment for *Fortune* magazine, to show the lives of white tenant farmers. Whereas Lorca had no definite assignment for his trip to New York, his general mission was to study languages at Columbia University, and composing poems was incidental to that purpose.

Both texts look with care at people trying to lead meaningful lives while having no political freedom and no social independence. Particularly in the case of *Famous Men*, the farmers and their families are bound, quite literally through contractual arrangements with their landlords, to the system that suppresses them. To understand Agee's feelings for the families he stays with, one need only consider this portion of a nearly page-long sentence:

---

[4] Lorca, "The Ballad of the Three Rivers," in *Collected Poems*, ed. Christopher Maurer (New York: Farrar, Straus, and Giroux, 2002), 97, ll. 7–8.

...how each of you is a creature which has never in all time existed before, and which shall never in all time exist again and which is not quite like any other and which has the grand stature and natural warmth of every other and whose existence is all measured upon a still mad and incurable time; how am I to speak of you as "tenant" "farmers," as "representatives" of your "class," as social integers in a criminal economy, or as individuals, fathers, mothers, sons, daughters, as my friends and as I "know" you?[5]

The interests of Agee and Lorca merge together most revealingly in their shared senses of intense moral empathy with individuals trampled upon by a generalizing social and economic system. Yet both men were ambivalent about Communism, and even though Lorca was murdered by the Fascist supporters of General Franco, he never openly expressed his political sympathies. Both writers resisted doctrinal belief systems and instead found truth in the perceptual energies and attentions of the invested individual.

Lorca's *Poet in New York* takes a hard look at economic and spiritual malaise, but the book opens with a sequence of warm, nostalgic childhood poems, suggesting the gentleness of the poet's origins. The tone—which is very much in the vein of Agee's "Knoxville: Summer of 1915"—that develops from the opening section of *Poet in New York*, in such poems as "1910 (Intermezzo)" and "Your Childhood in Menton," conveys only Lorca's version of the *Songs of Innocence* and not yet the *Songs of Experience*. The poem "1910 (Intermezzo)" begins:

Those eyes of mine in nineteen ten
saw no one dead and buried,
no village fair of ash from the one who weeps at dawn
no trembling heart cornered like a sea horse.[6]

The speaker of the poem has seen no suffering, no loss, nothing of what adulthood would later reveal. Lorca calls this opening section of *Poet in New York*, the first of ten numbered sections, "Poems of Solitude at Columbia University." These poems show a foreign student reflecting on

[5] Agee and Evans, *Famous Men*, 84.
[6] Lorca, "1910 (Intermezzo)," in *Poet in New York*, ed. Christopher Maurer (New York: Farrar, Straus, and Giroux, 1998), 7, ll. 1–4.

the homeland he has left behind and taking stock of the simplicities of his past before addressing a difficult present.

In Section II of the book, titled "The Blacks," Lorca's speaker is a grown man, already world-weary, looking out at the world in all its disorienting unfairness. He feels great empathy for the African American residents of New York City, whom he sees as trying to live authentic lives under the altering power of the white social and economic world:

> They hate the bird's shadow
> on the white cheek's high tide
> and the conflict of light and wind
> in the great cold hall of snow.
>
> They hate the unbodied arrow
> the punctual handkerchief of farewell,
> the needle that sustains a rosy tension
> in the seed-bearing spikes of their smiles.[7]

Lorca studies the hidden feelings of the African Americans, the anxiety and oppression they feel in a world in which they are not at home, are not even welcome guests. The image of the "bird's shadow" presents a most disturbing aspect of their lives in twentieth century America, a place where even Nature cannot be trusted and the makers of beautiful songs may very well betray them. Agee makes similar observations about the lives of African Americans in *Famous Men*, most poignantly during a scene in which he addresses a young couple walking on the road and feels shame and horror that he has both frightened them and made them aware of their own vulnerability.[8]

Both *Famous Men* and *Poet in New York* take a dark view of the multitude of ways capitalism ravages the poor. Agee's assigned project was to consider the lives of ordinary white sharecroppers, whereas Lorca is most struck in New York City by the culture of African Americans who live in a kind of urban poverty the poet has never witnessed before. Agee represented the people of his study in a nearly hyper-realistic manner, down to the worn threads of their garments. Lorca, on the other hand, often depicts

---

[7] Lorca, "The Blacks," in *Poet in New York*, 21, ll. 1–8.
[8] Agee and Evans, *Famous Men*, 34–36.

his human subjects in more abstract ways, as in these lines from "Blind Panorama of New York":

> Everyone understands the pain that accompanies death,
> but genuine pain doesn't live in the spirit,
> nor in the air, nor in our lives,
> not on these terraces of billowing smoke.
> The genuine pain that keeps everything awake
> is a tiny, infinite burn
> on the innocent eyes of other systems.[9]

Lorca pulls back from the physical and tactile suffering found in poems from earlier sections of the book, such as "Dance of Death" and "Landscape of a Vomiting Multitude (Dusk at Coney Island)." This speaker seems to say that the real source of human suffering is so far outside our control that it belongs to an entirely different system than the one we recognize, with the "tiny, infinite burn" suggesting a cosmic force at work. The poem concludes with an image of the Earth, as if seen from within and also at a great distance: "There is no pain in the voice. Only the Earth exists here. / The Earth and its timeless doors / which lead to blush of the fruit."[10]

The study of poetics goes back to Aristotle and continues from the earliest thinkers about literature to the most current. Jonathan Culler has defined poetics as "the attempt to account for literary effects by describing the conventions and reading operations that make them possible."[11] This definition is in keeping with the rhetorical and linguistic approaches to poetics that became prominent in the last quarter of the twentieth century. A poetics involves more than simply a style or a sensibility; a poetics comprises a perspective toward or upon its subject. In this regard, it encompasses more of a way of being, or "a way of seeing" (to reference Agee's work with the photographer Helen Levitt[12]), than a particular method or approach. Both style and sense occur within it, and it reaches after some

---

[9] Lorca, "Blind Panorama of New York," in *Poet in New York*, 67, ll. 11–17.

[10] Ibid., 69, ll. 43–47.

[11] Jonathan Culler, *Literary Theory: A Very Short Introduction*, (London: Oxford University Press, 1997), 66.

[12] Helen Levitt and James Agee, *A Way of Seeing: Photographs of New York* (New York: Viking, 1965).

level of essential being. Such an ontological matter is more difficult to demonstrate than aspects of method or elements of common ideological purpose, though these are two avenues of evidence for establishing a shared poetics.

The poetics of Agee and Lorca do not intertwine or intersect at any precise points but instead move along parallel lines throughout their writing lives. These parallel poetics involve both stylistic and ideological matters; while Agee and Lorca both tended to be flamboyant stylists, perhaps excessive at times in their descriptive inclinations, they were also deeply concerned with the lives of others and with giving value to the unappreciated. They perceived themselves as outsiders, especially in *Let Us Now Praise Famous Men* and *Poet in New York*, and that willingness to think beyond the mainstream likely created a sense of relationship with avant-garde modes of expression. Even certain of their biographical likenesses indicate a parallel line of poetics, such as early musical talent, particularly on the piano, and close associations with visual artists (Walker Evans and Helen Levitt for Agee; Salvador Dali for Lorca) and especially with filmmakers (Charlie Chaplin, John Huston, and Charles Laughton for Agee; Luis Bunuel for Lorca). Agee and Lorca arrived at strikingly similar conclusions about causes of suffering and degradation of life that came at the hands of oppressive political systems. They each hoped to represent humble lives, and the folkways that surround them, with a complex and often abstract artistic vision and through similar stylistic approaches, which were highly divergent from the earlier works of each. Both were lyrical writers, given to intensely detailed descriptions of their surroundings, often in the elevated sensory world of poetic language.

Agee made an attempt to show kinship between experimentalism and political art in his 1936 *New Masses* review of Gertrude Stein's "Geographical History of America, Or the Relation of Human Nature to the Human Mind."[13] Agee does not mention Stein even once after the opening sentence, but he does make a case for the revolutionary value of "[t]he material of dreams and the fluid subconscious, irrationalism, the electrically intense perception and representation of 'real' 'materials.'"[14] He does hold up James Joyce, and several early Russian filmmakers, as models of the social

---

[13] Agee, "Geographical History of America, Or the Relation of Human Nature to the Human Mind," review, *New Masses*, December 15, 1936, 48.

[14] Ibid.

relevance of experimental art, claiming, "[f]or the materials of so-called surrealism are the commonest of human property. And a man who cannot by mischance grasp a problem intellectually is grasped by it if it is presented through the subtler, more forceful, and more primitive logic of movement, timing, space, and light."[15] Agee appears untroubled by the paradox of aligning subtlety on the one hand with force and primitivism on the other. These manners might seem contradictory, but Agee's own writing makes them complementary.

One of the more compelling parallels between Agee and Lorca arises from a shared desire to incorporate poetic means that appear at odds with one another. Both writers undeniably absorbed elements of High Modern avant-garde movements, particularly surrealism and imagism, and even some of the darker notes of Dadaism. This fact alone does not set Agee and Lorca apart from many writers of the 1920s and 1930s. The influence of the avant-garde was pervasive, even among writers who did not embrace these approaches as their primary style. Agee and Lorca are distinctive, however, in their shared commitment to representing real human voices in their work, which bound them to some degree of verisimilitude. Realism of this type was strictly antithetical to the principles of the avant-garde, yet essential to Agee and to Lorca. Like Agee, Lorca began as a much more traditionalist poet than his later work suggests. Early poems by Lorca are modeled on ballads of Spanish folk music and on the late Symbolist style of Juan Ramon Jimenez. For Lorca, verisimilitude found a more comfortable home in his dramatic plays. Both Agee and Lorca eventually embrace an oratorical style, incorporating a voice of high dramatic tension. Both were interested in the sonorities of native speech, of the plain and unaffected, but also in the flourish of high literary manner. Agee's most lyrical writing appears in the prose of *Famous Men*, where the textural and sonic effects of language far surpass what he accomplished in his poetry. An example of this style, recalling the oratorical flare of Thomas Wolfe's prose, can be found in a lengthy passage describing the front bedroom of the Gudgers' house:

> At this certain time of late morning, then, in the full breadth of summer, here in this dark and shuttered room, through a knothole near the sharp crest of the roof, a signal or designation is made each day in silence and unheeded. A long bright rod of light takes to its

---

[15] Ibid., 50.

end, on the left side of the mantel, one of the small vases of milky and opalescent glass; in such a way, through its throat, and touching nothing else, that from within its self this tholed phial glows its whole shape on the obscurity, a sober grail, or divinity local to this home; and no one watches it, this archaic form, and alabastrine pearl, and captured paring of the phosphor moon, in what inhuman piety and silent fear it shows: and after a half minute it is faded and is changed, and is only a vase with light on it, companion of a never-lighted twin, and they stand in wide balance on the narrow shelf; and now the light has entirely left it, and oblates its roundness on the keen thumbprint of pine wall beside it, and this, slowly, slides, in the torsion of the engined firmament, while the round rind of the planet runs in its modulations like a sea, and along faint Oregon like jackstrewn matches, the roosters startling flame from one an-other, the darkness is lifted, a steel shade from a storefront.[16]

The breathless force of such writing is Agee at his most poetic, his most connected to the historical weight of the language of poetry. A phrase like "tholed phial" sounds as though it comes straight from *Beowulf* and from the same rough and elemental world in which *Beowulf* slays Grendel, a world in which the houses might not be so very different from the tenant house inhabited by the Gudger family in Alabama in 1936.

Lorca's style in *Poet in New York* could be similarly breathless, with the poems often written in long irregular lines and with infrequent punc-tuation. The presentation of the lines in such a manner gives the appear-ance of unbounded thoughts and feelings, a poet driven by a headlong Muse. One example can be found in the following lines from the poem "Crucifixion":

Blood flowed down the mountain and the angels looked for it,
but the chalices became wind and finally filled the shoes.
Crippled dogs puffed on their pipes and the odor of hot leather
grayed the round lips of those who vomited on street corners.
and long southern howls arrived with the arid night.
It was the moon burning the horse's phallus with its candles.[17]

---

[16] Agee and Evans, *Famous Men*, 163–64.
[17] Lorca, "Crucifixion," in *Poet in New York*, 145, ll. 4–9.

Both Agee and Lorca cited the importance of Walt Whitman, and he is the presiding influence over the style and voice of *Poet in New York* and many sections of *Famous Men*. One of the better-known poems from *Poet in New York* is called "Ode to Walt Whitman," in which Lorca pays tribute to Whitman's vision and courage, despite taking a much darker view of America and its culture of destruction and greed.

The middle-to-late Modernist period in Europe and America marks an ever-amalgamated search for forms commensurate to increasingly diverse subject material, following the radical approaches of surrealism, cubism, and other avant-garde movements, including James Joyce's "mythical method," as T.S. Eliot called it, for depicting day-in-the-life happenings through the lens of classical mythology. The spirit of the age for 1930s American writing was to embrace whatever means were at hand, to stretch the confines of genre, and to bring as many new voices into literature as possible. John Steinbeck and Clifford Odets, for instance, both sought to incorporate the perspectives of poor and working-class citizens who found little representation in the High Modernism of the 1920s. The long poem experienced a particularly vivid renaissance at the time, with the early stages Ezra Pound's *Cantos*, Eliot's *The Waste Land*, and other experiments that more resembled Lorca, such as Hart Crane's *The Bridge*, and the more Agee-like documentary style of early sections of William Carlos Williams's *Paterson*.

In the chapter *"Famous Men* as Surrealist Ethnography,"* from *The Making of James Agee*, Hugh Davis works out much of the context for the surrealist impulse in Agee's writings from the 1930s, particularly his techniques in *Famous Men*. Davis says,

> While Agee insists that art is incapable of reproducing experience, he does not give up on aesthetics altogether. Like the surrealists, he seeks to integrate the conscious and unconscious and to collapse boundaries between aesthetic categories not so much that art will cease to exist, but that art and life will become one.[18]

Agee shows this tendency often in describing the objects that decorate the lives of the Gudgers, the Ricketts, and the Woods. He does a great

---

[18] Hugh Davis, *The Making of James Agee* (Knoxville: University of Tennessee Press, 2008), 115. Davis goes into useful detail about the intertwining of Agee's aesthetic ideas and his political ones, examining also the contexts for surrealism within the political climate of the 1930s.

deal of Whitmanesque cataloguing of the items found in their houses and often employs techniques that show the objects as they appear, but not necessarily in a form recognizable to a reader who has not been there in person to see what Agee sees. He shows a clipping from a Birmingham, Alabama, newspaper, clearly not saved for the story it once told but for some other, unspecified purpose, likely more practical to the livelihood of the household. The image is rendered as follows:

GHAM NEWS
hursday afternoon, March 5, 1936
Price: 3 cents   .
     in G
     (else

Thousa
are on d
througho
cording its

for the Birm

(over two photographs:)
Glass and night sticks fly in[19]

The imagery continues in that way for several pages, with prose digressions interspersed in regular paragraph form. This looks very like the collage approach used in surrealist writings and also offers a fractured version of the Imagist style of an earlier decade. Agee finds an unsentimental method with which to present an emotional subject and to powerfully, but obliquely, suggest the manifold gaps and absences in the lives of his human subjects.

As a postscript that would have seemed unlikely at the times of their deaths, literary and popular culture has embraced both writers. James Agee has been recognized as one of the great screenwriters of his era, and a seminal film critic. A selected volume of his film criticism, *Agee on Film*, was chosen by legendary film director Martin Scorsese for his *Modern Library:*

---

[19] Agee and Evans, *Famous Men*, 138.

The Movies book series. Federico García Lorca inspired songs by artists as diverse and esteemed as Tim Buckley, Leonard Cohen, The Pogues, and punk rock icons The Clash, as well as a Hollywood film, *Death in Granada*. In fact, Joe Strummer of The Clash traveled to Granada to search for the site of Lorca's grave in 1984, buying shovels and recruiting friends to help him dig, though like the many who tried before him, Strummer found no grave for Lorca.[20]

International literary figures also continue to hold Agee and Lorca in high regard. The Norwegian novelist Karl Ove Knausgaard clearly paid homage to Agee by borrowing one of his book titles. The first installment of Knausgaard's 2009 six-volume autobiographical novel *My Struggle* is called *A Death in the Family* in European editions. French philosopher Jacques Rancière designates "Hale County, 1936-New York, 1941" as a major aesthetic site in his 2013 book, *Aisthesis: Scenes from the Aesthetic Regime of Art*. He titles his chapter "The Cruel Radiance of What Is" after a line from Agee's *Famous Men*. Rancière says, "It is only possible to account for these lives and their place in the world, however slightly, by going beyond the significant relation between the particular and the general towards the symbolic relation of the part to the unrepresentable whole that expresses its actuality."[21] That the symbolic relations of the parts, namely the images, to the wholes, the experiences embodied, are still subjects for discussion in the works of Agee and in Lorca's New York poems surely speaks to the lasting nature of the work they accomplished and suggests the influence that work will maintain in the future.

[20] Giles Tremlett, "Joe Strummer to Be Honoured with Square in Spanish City Granada," *The Guardian*, January 15, 2013, http://www.theguardian.com/music/2013/jan/15/joe-strummer-square-granada.

[21] Jacques Rancière, *Aisthesis: Scenes from the Aesthetic Regime of Art* (London, New York: Verso, 2013), 250.

PART 5

14. Surveying the Land of the Word: Nine Reviews

Charles Wright, *Oblivion Banjo*: *The Poetry of Charles Wright* (2020)

Oblivion Banjo, the new collection from former U.S. Poet Laureate Charles Wright, offers the first comprehensive survey of one of the major bodies of work in American poetry. Wright was born in Pickwick Dam, west Tennessee, in 1935 and spent most of his childhood in the northeastern Tennessee city of Kingsport. He has been recognized with most of the major awards and distinctions in the poetry world, including the Pulitzer Prize, the National Book Award, and the Bollingen Prize. Wright spent time between college degrees in the U.S. Army, which took him abroad to Italy, among other places, where he found inspiration to write poetry. He eventually taught writing at the University of California-Irvine, and later at the University of Virginia. Wright is the only U.S. Poet Laureate thus far whose poetry is associated with the region of Appalachia. *Oblivion Banjo* brings together Wright's own selection of the work he wants to preserve from a writing career that spans nearly half a century, and at more than 700 pages, it will be the volume that determines his permanent place in American literature.

Wright has been recognized for being worldly, even cosmic, in his subject matter, which makes the persistence of his Tennessee settings striking and purposeful. Tennessee locations and happenings are present from the earliest of Wright's individual volumes, *Hard Freight* from 1973, to the latest, *Caribou* from 2014. The Tennessee poems especially resonate because they are some of Wright's most personal writing and reveal more of his background and family life than poems set in other locations. For instance, in the long poem I think of as his signature piece, "The Southern Cross" (from the 1981 volume of the same title), the speaker relates a memory from earliest childhood:

All day I've remembered a lake and a sudsy shoreline,
Gauze curtains blowing in and out of open windows all over the South.

It's 1936, in Tennessee. I'm one
And spraying the dead grass with a hose.
The curtains blow in and out.

And then it's not. And I'm not and they're not.

The poem resists the nostalgia of continuity, and the speaker seems to distrust his own recollections at times, indicating how selective memory can be and how we often want to create a story line where one does not exist. "The Southern Cross" takes us to different points in time, and across the world to Italian gardens, English cemeteries, the coastline of Ischia, and summer "in the high Montana air," before circling back to the hills above Kingsport and finally to the place of origin, remembered in the poem's final section as such:

Pickwick was never the wind....

It's what we forget that defines us, and stays
     in the same place,
And waits to be rediscovered.
Somewhere in all that network of rivers and roads and silt hills,
A city I'll never remember,
               its walls the color of pure light,
Lies in the August heat of 1935,
In Tennessee, the bottomland slowly becoming a lake.

While Charles Wright has been a beloved poet for decades, his poetry may still feel remote to readers new to his work. Reading Wright's poems could be thought of as the process of observing an illuminated mind in conversation with the people, places, books, and beliefs that have made an impact upon it. A reader doesn't have to know everything in the Bible, or Dante, or the ancient Chinese poets, as extensively as Charles Wright knows them to comprehend how much they have shaped his experience. The brilliance of Wright's achievement lies in how seamlessly he integrates such cultural monuments with everyday occurrences that almost anyone can relate to, like sitting in the backyard and watching clouds pass overhead, or reflecting on one's travels, or simply remembering moments from childhood that refuse to be forgotten. *Oblivion Banjo* reveals the evolution and expansion of a singular voice, a singular vision, through the stages of a closely observed and considered life.

Though I have studied Charles Wright's poetry since I was an undergraduate at The University of Tennessee, at the prescient suggestion of the late Dr. Arthur Smith, I confess I was still taken aback by the power of reading these poems all together. I find a mystery in them that reminds me of Emily Dickinson, a glorious fecundity to the language that makes me think of Gerard Manley Hopkins, and a painterly attention to the smallest movements and stillnesses that brought Wallace Stevens continually to mind. Yet Charles Wright has developed his own style, a characteristic use of lineation and diction that no regular reader of poems could mistake for any other poet, and a manner of delivering and developing his meditations that is truly original. *Oblivion Banjo* offers moments of harrowing existential dread, luminous beauty, and wry humor, and these qualities combine with the title to suggest that eternity is a reality beyond conception, but that there is no reason not to face it with a bit of hopeful music.

Robert D. Denham, *Charles Wright: A Companion to the Late Poetry, 1988–2007* (2009)

In 1983, the poet Charles Wright left a distinguished faculty position at The University of California-Irvine to return to the region of his upbringing and teach at the University of Virginia. He has since established Appalachia as a cornerstone of his subject matter, having written a series of poems titled "Appalachian Book of the Dead" and individual poems called "Appalachian Farewell," "Appalachian Lullaby," and "Appalachia Dog." Wright even gave his 1998 book the title *Appalachia*. When his most recent poetry collection, *Littlefoot*, came out in 2007, prominent reviews appeared in the *Los Angeles Times* and the *New York Review of Books*, in which the esteemed poetry critic Helen Vendler lauded Wright's work as so true and believable that it seems to have been "miraculously snatched from the air." No other poet from Appalachia, and perhaps the entire American South, so regularly receives this kind of national coverage.

Despite his embrace of his Appalachian roots in such a remarkable way, Wright's poetry presents a paradox. He has written beautifully of the people and the environment of the region, yet he also resists many of the hallmarks of both Southern and Appalachian writing, such as a sense of narrative development and a concern with the long-lasting effects of history as it relates to place. His landscape poems are more often focused on his backyard and the constellations of the night sky than on the wilds of the Appalachian forests or mountains. The poetry of Charles Wright presents a reader with a special set of difficulties, including a broad range of literary and visual arts references, a reliance on often discontinuous images, and a speaker who does not always locate the reader in time and space. This is where Robert D. Denham's wonderful book, *Charles Wright: A Companion to the Late Poetry, 1988–2007*, becomes so useful. Denham provides studies and commentaries for all 265 poems Wright has collected in books since *Chickamauga* in 1995. Denham identifies the overarching

shape of Wright's work as "a variation on the quest narrative," and each
poem constitutes an important thread within the context of Wright's lifelong poetic pilgrimage.

The structure of Denham's book might appear daunting at first, with
its use of Aristotelian terminology and geometrical diagrams in the introduction. Do not be discouraged. Denham applies these tools to establish a
clear and direct method for systematically placing and interpreting each of
Wright's poems. The language of Aristotle's *Poetics* provides Denham with
a classic foundation for discussing the components of poetry and ultimately
bestows a timeless quality on Wright's work. To regard the full value of
Denham's scholarship, one needs only to consider a passage from his treat-
ment of a fairly difficult Wright poem, such as "Umbrian Dreams," from
one of his most celebrated books, *Black Zodiac*:

> In the first line we have a sort of negative metaphor. Nothing is
> flat-lit: everything is brilliant and fully lit. Nothing is tabula-rasaed:
> everything is fully inscribed. The landscape, which previously had
> been like the green heart of Italy, has not been changed into an
> Umbrian sackcloth, but into a brilliant autumn spectacle, as colorful
> as a Mycenaean mask. In such a lush and spectacular setting, where
> the October backdrop is like that of a fully-adorned drag queen,
> somber thoughts of the crucifixion implied by the stigmata and the
> *Stabat mater* are distant ("a sleep and a death away").

Denham also provides thorough footnotes for three potentially obscure references in the poem: *tabula rasa* (Locke's blank slate of mind,
which Wright transforms into a past participle verb form); *Umbria* (a ver-
dant region in Italy); and *Stabat mater* (the opening words of a thirteenth
century hymn in the Stations of the Cross ceremony). Denham captures
every aspect of the poem's achievement, from its descriptive power to its
meditative fluidity. Denham is equally capable in situating and explicating
some of Wright's more expansive pieces, such as the fragmentary lyrics of
"Buffalo Yoga" and its three "Coda" poems from *Buffalo Yoga* (2004), and
the numbered sequence of poems that make up *Littlefoot* (2007).

Charles Wright is one of a handful of contemporary Appalachian poets who is likely to be read in a hundred years, and the need for an accomplished body of critical work to accompany the poetry is increasingly apparent. Just as Virgil guides Dante through the labyrinths of the
underworld, Denham knowledgeably leads the way for any reader looking
to fully engage Charles Wright's poetry. An interesting aspect of Wright's

poetry is that it is so enjoyable to a general reader, despite the heavy use of reference and allusion: the poems are filled with observations about and descriptions of everyday experiences seen in fresh ways; they are immersed in the important larger questions of life and the afterlife that readers of poetry hope to find; and they are written in a voice and style so generous and charming that one feels invited into the speaker's vision of the world. Anyone who appreciates poetry at all can enjoy Wright's poems, but for a reader looking to gain a more comprehensive grasp of the work, Denham's book will become a permanent companion to it, in much the way that Don Gifford's famous *Annotated* now stands beside James Joyce's *Ulysses*. A second volume, *The Early Poetry of Charles Wright: A Companion, 1960–1990*, will complete Denham's study of nearly a half century's work by Wright; taken together, Denham's two *Companion* books will serve as the definitive guide to the work of a major American poet.

Southern Appalachian Poetry: An Anthology of Works by 37 Poets, edited by Marita Garin (2009)

There can be little doubt that the past decade has brought a renewed and invigorated interest in writing from the Appalachian region. Most of that attention, and the critical discussion surrounding it, has centered on works of fiction, particularly novels such as Robert Morgan's *Gap Creek* and Charles Frazier's *Cold Mountain* that have reached a broad international readership. An earlier generation of books, such as James Still's *River of Earth* and Harriette Arnow's *The Dollmaker*, are often written about and taught in classrooms and are now rightly recognized as classics. With the arrival of *Southern Appalachian Poetry*, Marita Garin has provided a long-needed opportunity to appreciate the overshadowed but exceedingly vibrant poetry this region has produced.

Garin includes a fine introductory chapter to *Southern Appalachian Poetry*, one that considers common images and tendencies that unify this diverse collection of poems. Many poems in the anthology reflect on the predominant themes of the region (and of American poetry in general for the past seventy years), such as family life, landscape, and the relation of an individual to his or her local history. New readers of Appalachian poetry, however, may be surprised by the sense of humor that permeates so much of the work, such as "Remodeling the Hermit's Cabin" by Fred Chappell and "The Brier Losing Touch with His Traditions" by Jim Wayne Miller. These two poems play on the classic comic trope of foiling expectations, in each case regional stereotypes—Chappell's poem begins with the fragment, "Not what we expected." The voices in the anthology show great variety, ranging from the humorous to the poignant. In an age when the national media tends to paint the political life of Appalachia in broad strokes, as a unified voting bloc, the book's many poems on the grinding effects of poverty and coal mining are a welcome reminder that we residents of the region also maintain a powerful voice of resistance.

All readers of Appalachian literature will welcome the excellent selections of poems from writers such as Don Johnson and Louise McNeill, whose works have been inexplicably under-read. After considering Johnson's "Going Home" and McNeill's "The Roads," a reader might feel something close to outrage at the insubstantial poems now so frequently published in *Poetry* magazine and *The New Yorker*. These poems stand well alongside contemporary classics like "Trillium" by Kathryn Stripling Byer, "The Gift of Tongues" by Robert Morgan, and "Dog Creek Mainline" by Charles Wright, as well as work by James Still and George Scarbrough. The cumulative effect of bringing such poems together is stirring, as though the land, the customs, and the ghostly endurance of the past have asserted themselves through the various tones and images, a testament to the native genius of place expressed through individual voices.

If *Southern Appalachian Poetry* falters in any way, the shortcoming is that the anthology feels too limited in time and scope. It doesn't go back into the past far enough to suffice as the definitive, comprehensive anthology of Appalachian poetry that so many readers and teachers would like to have. No poems are included from such significant early poets as Jesse Stuart, Byron Herbert Reece, or Emma Bell Miles. Conversely, the book was published in 2008, yet it represents hardly any poets whose first works emerged after 1995, so it also is not an effective snapshot of the contemporary life of Appalachian poetry. These issues are gracefully explained in the book's preface, but still the absences loom large. For example, in the case of Jeff Daniel Marion, not a single poem appears from what is arguably his strongest single collection, *Letters Home*, from 1999, and only one that appeared after 1990, thus representing only a fraction of an illustrious thirty-five-year career. Poets such as Maurice Manning, Michael Chitwood, and Lynn Powell have written some of the finest poems to appear anywhere in the past decade, yet their work is not in the anthology. Similarly, there are no poets of color in *Southern Appalachian Poetry*, though the contributions of Frank X. Walker and other Affrilachian poetry movement writers comprise an undeniably important chapter in the literature of the region.

McFarland & Company deserves considerable praise for their *Contributions to Southern Appalachian Studies* series, which for more than a decade has brought out a fascinating collection of books. Marita Garin also has offered a valuable service to the study of Appalachian literature and stopped a gap that has been open for too long. *Southern Appalachian Poetry* is a rewarding and pleasurable book, with the personalizing touch of the author's photographs as well as autobiographical sketches in which the poets discuss their influences, inspirations, and life histories. The need remains for both a comprehensive anthology of Appalachian poetry from its beginnings and a collection that would provide a picture of what is happening at present in poetry from the region. For now, though, we have many reasons to celebrate the arrival of this handsome anthology and to appreciate the fine poets whose work makes up its contents.

Linda Parsons Marion, *Mother Land: Poems* (2010)

Many readers of Linda Parsons Marion's 1997 debut poetry collection, *Home Fires*, have anxiously awaited more of the hand-crafted images of family and youth that were the signature of that book. With the arrival of Marion's *Mother Land*, our hopefulness has been rewarded with a book that surpasses the accomplishment of the earlier work. The poems in *Mother Land* stand alone as rich and graceful lyrics, but taken together they unfold both a narrative and a theme about healing oneself through nurturing the soil. The underlying narrative of *Mother Land* tells of a young girl's difficult childhood with an unstable mother and a charming but detached father, both more absorbed in their own lives than with the daughter who slips through their fingers. The theme of the book, that the tending required for keeping a garden is equally necessary for maintaining even the closest human relationships, infuses the narrative with an overarching purpose as well as a sense of beauty and mystery.

Mother Land opens with the prologue-poem "Credo," which offers the unforgettable line "I believe in the bicycle of forgiveness" and recounts many of the joys and hurts of childhood. "Credo" introduces the people who figure so prominently throughout the book, especially the mother whom she both chose and did not choose, whose "misfiring in your head, manic / depressive charge / that drove me through Alice's looking-glass, under quilts / behind chairs until stormclouds lifted." We get to know the mother throughout the book, in such poems as "Letter to My Mother" and "Diagnosis," and the father as well, in "Self-Addressed" and "Shirt Tail." In "Rescue," we learn of the saving grace of a kindly stepmother, just the opposite of the fairytale version, who takes in the wounded young girl, "among the broken-winged / and lame who sniff her out, homing right to her touch." Marion balances the range of these poems by guiding us through the far country of her childhood and into the near country of her own parenting (conveyed beautifully in the book's cover art, painted by her daughter Rachel, which depicts an image of blooming and entangling that deserves its own essay).

Digging in the earth as a means for self-discovery is a metaphor associated with male poets seeking to understand the agricultural lives of their fathers, and one may think of Seamus Heaney's famous early poem "Digging," as well as the soil-labor in Wendell Berry's poetry, more than once while reading *Mother Land*. Yet the search in these poems is for the mother, just as elusive and terrifying at times as the father-figure, submerged in the world of the greenhouse, in Theodore Roethke's poems. Marion chooses passages from Roethke's *Words for the Wind* as epigraphs for the sections of her book, which serve as a perfect touchstone for the quest undertaken in *Mother Land*. Greenhouses and gardens suggest a different kind of cultivation than open fields and furrows. The work happens nearer to the domestic space of the house and its interiors, crafted by hand and left less to the elements. Marion's poems display a command of economy and form without feeling sparse or tight; they move through a variety of stanza forms and tonal registers with a consistent generosity of voice. The book closes with two poems, "This Digging" and "Ground Time," which elucidate the pleasure and renewal to be found in the soil, in turning life out of the complex dirt, seen clearly in the book's final lines: "While the Earth ends one day barren, steaming / in ancient argument, it wakes beloved with child, / this ground, this slow brew of time."

In the 2000s, two women poets from the South won the Pulitzer Prize in poetry with second books that develop theme and narrative through connected lyric poems; Linda Parsons Marion's *Mother Land* stands shoulder to shoulder with Claudia Emerson's *Late Wife* and Natasha Trethewey's *Native Guard*, both in the strength and particularity of individual poems and in the largeness of vision that links the whole collection. Like Georgics of the emotional terrain, Marion's poems not only seek but also instruct, though their instructions are not didactic or directly stated. One can learn from these poems how to re-seed misused ground, to heal damaged realms of the spirit, and to plant new life where old life has withered. Linda Parsons Marion's work ranges broadly across time and deeply into the earth to find the richest resources for examining a fully perceived life. Ralph Waldo Emerson said, "The line of beauty is the line of perfect economy," and the poems in *Mother Land* prove this idea as well any written today.

Charles Dodd White, *Lambs of Men* (2012)

The Gothic tradition is alive and well in contemporary American literature. A strong argument could be made that the Gothic is at the very center
of our literary canon, dating back to perhaps the first truly distinctive
American writer, Edgar Allan Poe. The lineage encompasses most of Nathaniel Hawthorne, many elements of Herman Melville, and much of the
lasting literature from the American South, from William Faulkner and
Flannery O'Connor to Cormac McCarthy and William Gay. Charles
Dodd White's first novel, *Lambs of Men*, makes a distinguished new addition to this long and fascinating tradition. Many classic elements of the
Gothic are at play in *Lambs of Men*: an act of inconceivable brutality within
the sacred bounds of family life; a community's sense of both horror and
curiosity as the details unfold; an accumulating dread that the evil at the
heart of such an event can never be explained. White's remarkable talent
as a storyteller holds these elements together in a fresh and suspenseful
tale, an original take on a well-established genre.

Lambs of Men presents a story of aftermath: the effects of World War
I, the accidental death of a child, the suicide of a wife and mother, and the
impact of a heinous crime against a child that stuns a mountain community. The main character is a United States Marine Corps veteran named
Hiram Tobit, who returns to his home in the mountains of western North
Carolina to work as a recruiter for the Corps. Tobit has seen the horrors
of war in France and has mixed feelings about bringing other mountain
boys into the field of such prospects. As the novel opens, he is estranged
from his family, his community, and his profession. One of the many
pleasures of reading *Lambs of Men* is watching Hiram's immersion back
into his former life unfold.

The novel moves well in an episodic structure, with crisp dialogue
between believable characters. The real strength of White's writing, however, is the prose style, which often reaches a poetic intensity of language
and imagery. This often happens in descriptions of landscape or physical
labor, as in Hiram's first trek back to his native lands:

The track they followed had been riven by long autumn rains and baked over with a winter sun, so that the ruts were deep and hazardous in the low light and fresh snow. Hiram let the horse move slow, feeling its way on the clay while he nodded in a half sleep.

As this passage demonstrates, White is often attuned not only to the appearance of nature but to its processes as well. He writes with a keen eye and a sharp ear to the way the natural world reveals itself to those who attend to it. There is frequently a metaphysical quality to the reflections on landscape, and certain characters seem more adept at hearing the voices that speak in whispers all around them.

As many characters in *Lambs of Men* discover, closeness to nature does not exempt one from suffering. This is a novel infused with pain. *Lambs of Men* offers enough bloodshed to ward off the squeamish, but the heart of the novel concerns a damaged relationship between a father and a son. Because of an accident he caused while his son Hiram was still a child, Sloane Tobit figures into the story well before his first appearance. Sloane becomes an important presence in Hiram's life again when both get involved in the search for the suspect of a terrible crime, also a father who has lost control of his feelings. White handles the difficult feelings between the father and the son with deep empathy and grace. Both characters make grievous mistakes and display serious flaws, especially when they deal with one another, yet they remain sympathetic as individuals. *Lambs of Men* poignantly considers the timeless question of whether two people who have caused each other great harm can still have a meaningful relationship.

If one were to point out the shortcoming of *Lambs of Men*, it would be literally that, at 159 pages, it clocks in as a fairly short book. The novel is so well written, and the development of the characters so interesting and persuasive, that one wishes it went on longer. White misses an opportunity to expand on the role of certain important characters, particularly the woman Cass, whom Hiram marries and with whom he is expecting the child that will further the troubled Tobit bloodline. Very little of their courtship happens in view of the reader, and even less of Cass's past, which includes a charming daughter, comes to light. The novel concludes beautifully, however, with a last look backward that allows a new perspective on a part of the past that caused much suffering for the Tobit family.

Charles Dodd White has emerged as one of the Appalachian region's most promising young fiction writers. Almost immediately following the appearance of *Lambs of Men*, and its subsequent notice as a finalist of the Weatherford Award for Fiction from the Appalachian Studies Association, White served as an editor for *Degrees of Elevation: Short Stories of Contemporary Appalachia*, an important new anthology. White and co-editor Page Seay bring together such well-established writers as Ron Rash and Silas House as well as rising stars like Mark Powell and John McManus. In addition to *Lambs of Men* and the short story anthology, White has a collection of his own short stories, *The Sinners of Sanction County*, due out from Bottom Dog Press in the fall of 2011. Following an accomplished first novel with such varied and significant production suggests that readers will hear more and more from the talented voice of Charles Dodd White.

Still in Print: The Southern Novel Today, edited by Jan Nordby Gretlund (2012)

At least since the days of Faulkner and the Southern Renaissance, the fortunes of Southern literature have risen and fallen on the success of its novels. That undoubtedly represents a golden age for the novel in the South, but the region's literature has continued to flourish into the present, and not simply as a hallmark of times past. While none of the novelists discussed here have the same iconic name recognition as Warren, Welty, or Wolfe (though McCarthy is increasingly a one-name figure), many of these writers have broad national audiences and awards among their credits. To make a current assessment of the South's most valuable literary commodity, Danish scholar Jan Nordby Gretlund has published an essay collection with an interesting premise: eighteen accomplished literary critics were asked to discuss a single Southern novel published since 1997 that they hope to see kept in print. The result is a group of essays, broadly ranging and deeply probing, with an introduction by Gretlund that indicates how the novelists encompass both the present sense of flux pervading the New South and the longing for a grasp on an ever-more-distant past.

The great pleasure of *Still in Print* lies in reading such distinguished scholars as Edwin T. Arnold, best known for plumbing the darker depths of Cormac McCarthy's novels considering the bizarre humor of the late Donald Harrington, and pondering M. Thomas Inge's examination of the origins of Charles Frazier's *Cold Mountain*. Gretlund made the excellent decision to invite choices from the most promising younger critics of Southern literature to stand alongside the more established readers. For example, Tara Powell's study of *Erasure*, Percival Everett's novel about an unexpected and counterintuitive form of racial discrimination, placed that novel at the top of my summer reading list. Even dedicated followers of the Southern novel are likely to find new and interesting suggestions for what to read from the expert scholars brought together in *Still in Print*.

From the perspective of Appalachian literary studies, however, *Still in Print* is a fair disappointment. As is often the case in scholarship on

Southern literature, the region of Appalachia feels seriously underrepresented. Only four of the eighteen novels could be considered Appalachian: Charles Frazier's *Cold Mountain*; Cormac McCarthy's *The Road*; Chris Offutt's *The Good Brother*; and Ron Rash's *One Foot in Eden*. Of these four, Frazier's novel takes place during the Civil War, McCarthy's occurs in a post-apocalyptic version of the future, and much of Offutt's takes place in the Pacific Northwest; only Rash fully addresses life in the recent past of Appalachia. Not coincidentally, one of the most valuable contributions in *Still in Print* is Thomas Ærvold Bjerre's essay on Rash's excellent first novel. Bjerre places *One Foot in Eden* in useful historical context, invoking James Fenimore Cooper, William Faulkner, and the Agrarian tradition in America, notably including the seminal work *Virgin Land: The American West as Symbol and Myth* by Henry Nash Smith.

Still in Print: The Southern Novel Today offers many individual rewards from its contributors, but not much of an overall direction. Gretlund doesn't claim to make a list of canonical works and then defend them. What are the eighteen best, or most important, or most interesting novels from the American South in the past fifteen years? That is an intriguing series of questions, but not one that *Still in Print* aspires to answer. Many of the novels included would be a part of that discussion, but without such books as Robert Morgan's *Gap Creek* (1999) and Silas House's *A Parchment of Leaves* (2002), just to name a couple of titles from the Appalachian region, the conversation feels incomplete. Appalachian fiction has become the engine that drives the Southern novel, and without a fuller representation of Appalachia, a definitive survey of the status of "the Southern novel today" just isn't possible. In the end, it's not clear whether *Still in Print* is trying to answer any pressing critical questions, though it is not a bad place to begin if the question is, "Which novel should I read next?"

Amy Greene, *Long Man* (2014)

In her much-anticipated second novel, *Long Man*, Amy Greene takes up the challenge of creating a fictional account of the removal of citizens from their homes by the Tennessee Valley Authority (TVA) in the mid-1930s. No other cultural event affected so many lives in rural East Tennessee, which is the setting of Greene's novel. The debate about the TVA remains unresolved after nearly eighty years, and recent incidents such as the coal ash spill of 2008 in Kingston, Tennessee, serve as reminders of the source of resistance to the institution. Was TVA removal a case of egregious government intrusion on private lives and private property, or was it a necessary sacrifice by some for the good of the many, a manageable consequence of progress for the common good? These issues are tangible in Greene's novel, but such political questions are present without overwhelming her attention to the characters and their experiences, which make *Long Man* such a memorable piece of writing.

Though many compelling characters populate *Long Man*, the presence of Annie Clyde Dodson dominates the novel. She is an independent young woman who lives with her husband and small daughter on the farm she inherited from her deceased parents. TVA agents fear her, and neighbors—before they left the condemned town of Yuneetah—seemed mostly confounded by her. She is not friendly or charming, not witty or eloquent. She is more like a force of nature: solitary, mindful, and above all, powerful. Her independence is all the more remarkable given the time and place in which the novel is set, and her role as a married woman is at odds with her husband about their future.

The character who most balances the novel, and provides a kind of antithesis to Annie Clyde Dodson, is a drifter named Amos who was raised in Yuneetah and returns to find it almost completely empty. Amos's motives are unclear from the beginning, just as Annie Clyde's motives—to remain on her land so that her daughter may experience the beauty and freedom of that world—are perfectly clear. Amos is diffuse, a man without articulate convictions, yet definitely compelled toward some unspoken goal in his trip back through the abandoned town of his youth. The new TVA dam, which has driven most everyone else away from the town, seems to have drawn Amos back toward it.

Greene subtly introduces the major dramatic event of the novel with an intensely gripping scene in which Annie Clyde and James Dodson slowly realize that their child, Gracie, has disappeared. Tension is built steadily as scene after scene shows the water rising in Yuneetah, with the Dodsons waiting until the last day to evacuate before it reaches dangerous levels. A real sense of panic instills the first pages of Gracie's disappearance and the foggy and rainy nighttime search that ensues. Annie Clyde incriminates Amos, and some of the interesting secondary characters, like her difficult aunt, Silver Ledford—who leads an isolated life as a bootlegger higher up in the ridges above Yuneetah—begin to play important roles.

None of the characters in *Long Man* are exactly likeable in any conventional way, except the child Gracie and faithful hound Rusty. This presents another remarkable aspect of the book: Greene avoids sentimentality without sacrificing sentiment. *Long Man* brings a world long past back into existence and fills it with characters and situations that are as complex as the world today.

Certain readers will likely feel that they have seen one too many lonely old granny women in mountain cabins who have a special "second sight," or one too many beaten-down but good-hearted sheriffs, in Appalachian fiction. Somewhere out there, an industrious graduate student surely is writing a dissertation called *Conflicted Lawmen in American Fiction*, and Greene's Ellard Moody would deserve a chapter alongside Cormac McCarthy's Ed Tom Bell from *No Country for Old Men* and Ron Rash's Will Alexander from *One Foot in Eden*. Moody could easily have been a flat character, or one that most readers have seen before, but in *Long Man*, the sheriff's devotion is not automatic, not assumed. He remains steadily unsure if he is doing anyone any good, and his nemesis Amos (whom Moody misreads, largely for personal reasons), certainly feels that Moody has failed the town he has sworn to protect. Such fine shadings prevent familiar characters types from feeling like stereotypes. The same point could be made for Beulah Kesterson, the granny woman in *Long Man*. She is solitary and frightening to the other characters for her "reading of the bones" she wears around her neck, but she also displays warmth and kindness toward the unloved Amos, whom she has raised since he was abandoned in childhood. There are no simple characters, or simple solutions, in *Long Man*, and that is part of what makes it so fascinating.

With *Long Man*, Amy Greene has accomplished the most difficult task of following up her hugely successful first novel *Bloodroot*. As a global bestseller that has been translated into several languages, while simultaneously being embraced in her native Appalachia, *Bloodroot* casts a deep shadow. But *Long Man* surpasses its predecessor in many ways. More sophisticated in style and structure than *Bloodroot*, the novel better sustains its tension and focus and is more emotionally resonant in its conclusions.

Long Man displays the growth of a serious artist. Greene has been praised for her lyricism, and while that is the quality that stands out most in her writing, *Long Man* develops a new clarity to counterbalance the lyrical beauty of the novel's language, and that makes a potent combination. Greene brings the past into a vivid contemporaneity, writing about lives and struggles that will be impossible for most readers to forget in a voice that is both intense and clear as her Silver Ledford's whiskey. *Long Man* delivers the happy message that one of America's most gifted young novelists is working right here, creating her art in the heart of Appalachia.

Jeff Daniel Marion, *Letters to the Dead: A Memoir* (2015)

During the past four decades, Jeff Daniel Marion has composed one of the central bodies of work in Appalachian literature. No full account can be taken of the region's poetry without looking closely at what Marion has accomplished, and recent years have seen his work recognized with a number of honors, including the James Still Award for Writing about the Appalachian South from the Fellowship of Southern Writers. Marion recently released his ninth collection of poems, *Letters to the Dead: A Memoir*, which has already won the 2013 Book of the Year Award in Poetry from the Appalachian Writers' Association. *Letters to the Dead* illuminates the importance of what one learns from those who have passed before us and also how much one might still have to say to them after their passing.

In these new poems, Marion brings together two primary modes of lyric poetry, the elegy and the ode, which have guided poets since the ancient Greeks. With their graceful imagery and moving family remembrances, the poems in *Letters to the Dead* convey a sense of mourning for those who have been lost and also a sense of joy at recalling the details of their lives. By calling this collection of poems *A Memoir*, Marion promises an unwavering look at what really happens between blood relations, at both the warmth and the tensions they share, and at how even long lives together maintain their secret spaces.

Letters to the Dead opens with one of Marion's strongest poems, "The Dying Art," whose title suggests some of the dual nature of the entire collection. The poem begins with the speaker on the surgeon's table, hearing the physician's phrase, "the zone of particularity," which reminds him of where the source of poems and letters is to be found. The "dying art" of the poem is the writing of letters, drafted out by hand with care and sent to an individual person. In an age of instant communication, the survival of such an art form seems imperiled, almost hopeless, and yet the speaker insists that no other means can convey what needs to be said. Here the poem introduces the theme for the entire book: "What I need to say is in that narrow / valley, the zone of what I had no chance / to say to all those long gone." He has already mastered the art of losing, and now he must say what needs to be said before he masters the art of those gone ahead, the art of dying. Poetry readers might think of T. S. Eliot's "patient etherized upon a table," Sylvia Plath's "Lady Lazarus," or Elizabeth Bishop's "One Art," and all those literary forebears are relevant for a collection of poems that looks backward to regain some footing in the present.

Many of the poems are addressed to particular relatives—aunts, uncles, grandparents—and some to eccentric or comic members of the poet's childhood community of Rogersville, Tennessee. Marion was the only child born from three marriages between Marion brothers and Gladson sisters, and the abundance of attention from such a childhood provides some of the comedy of these poems. Many of the most humorous involve stories by and about those relatives, such as "Aunt Verdie's Fountain of Youth" and "My Grandma Lucy Attends Her Own Funeral." The full range of Marion's voice finds an outlet in "The Tenant Farmer's Wife," told from the perspective of the poet's grandmother, Linnie Stubblefield Marion, born in 1883. This poem moves seamlessly between sharp-eyed wit and bleak realism about the uncertain circumstances of a young wife, then a young widow, in the early part of the twentieth century.

The most moving poems in *Letters to the Dead* are those addressed to the poet's parents. In 2009, Marion devoted an entire collection to poems about his father, J. D. Marion, simply called *Father*. Given that prior attention, the letter-poems directed to Eloise Gladson Marion, the poet's mother, are of special interest, particularly three poems in the middle of the book: "Sentimental Journey," "The Uninvited Guests," and "Fate." The poet recalls details from childhood, songs they sang together, and sayings shared among the family. The relationship explored is both warm and cool, both close and distant, and most touching when the poignancy of his mother's hardships is remembered: "surviving scarlet / fever, diphtheria, sentimental journey? / O who can understand the heart's yearnings?" Throughout a long career, in poem after poem and in this new volume particularly, Jeff Daniel Marion searches out the words and memories that help us all understand each heart's peculiar yearnings.

William Wright, Preface to *Grass Chapels: New & Selected Poems* (2021)

William Wright invokes the Muses. He writes visionary poems in the old sense, conjuring images from the deep subconscious—maybe the collective, maybe only his own. The poems sort and sift through the past, through near and distant memories, yet they feel alive and attuned to the present and mindful of the future. Wright's poems brim with the detailed specificity of his close observation of plants, animals, rocks, flowers in fields, water maneuvering between creek banks. He studies large-scale motifs (the cosmos), the micro-world (atomic and subatomic realities), and the complexities of all life. One encounters an almost microscopic examination of insects, like the yellow jacket and the cicada. Accurate recording alone, however, does not create memorable poems—details must be encompassed by a conceptual framework, an interrelating vision that adds depth and significance to the imagery. William Blake may have seen the world in this way, or Emily Dickinson adrift in her rooms, or Hart Crane late at night and in his cups. "Sing to me," Wright seems to beckon, "sing to me, O Muse, of spirits in high hidden coves and beneath the marshy shallows." The poems in *Grass Chapels* peer into the dark corners and empty halls of old barns, where the only life is small and trying to keep hidden. Spiders and moths, mice and the owls and foxes that hunt them, all have a home here. This work offers ruin and rebirth in near equal measure, and when rebirth is not possible remembrance must suffice.

The first set of poems I recall reading by William Wright included "Trumpet Creeper," which would appear in his second full-length collection, *Night Field Anecdote*. In the opening stanza, I encountered the phrase "Lacertilian armies" and reached for my trusted *American Heritage* dictionary. I kept reading and felt increasingly thrilled by the ambition of the language and the scope of the long and multifaceted poem. When I came to the lines "fields of ducts, white worms, smokestacks— / a trillion trillion cellular divinities," I sensed I was reading a poet informed by both hard-scientific learning and alchemy. Next I read "Blonde Mare, Iredell County, NC, 1870-1896," and was stunned by the tenderness of imagining the yoked hardship experienced by both the horse and its owners. The concluding lines of the poem show their final union more than a century later: "all knitted by death's / twine, your crux not lost but heaved by creek / and meadow, sluiced through the blowing manes of trees."

Lyricism is the primary mode in Wright's poetry, but many poems are driven by characters and their narratives. The selections from *Bledsoe* give the deepest immersion into a fictional world where disability and strained family ties bleed into a kind of violence normally associated with true crime drama. In later poems like "The Milk Witch," from *Tree Heresies*, Wright moves beyond folklore into the realm of folk horror, a genre more often discussed in film studies than literature. The image of "the season's rain / locked behind her smiling eyes" reminds us why we fear what happens in the dark, and why we suspect unnatural forces at work when crops fail and cows run dry. Anyone who reads of the furrow plowed by the blonde mare, or of the shrouded conjuring of the milk witch, will recognize the fine and distinctive thread William Wright has stitched into the flag of American poetry.

I hope readers will pursue *Grass Chapels* straight through and then go back and read it again in reverse. They will see the growth of the poet's mind, how certain themes were planted early and bloom into fullness throughout. The language of botany and geology are present from the beginning, as is the longing for deep and familial connection with the past. The earliest poems in the book, from *Dark Orchard*, may lack the formal or technical sophistication of the new poems, but they possess an undeniable brilliance in figuration and imagery. Poems such as "Dreaming of My Parents" reveal Wright's early desire to connect with places of origin and to commemorate the womb and the nest of our upbringing. When Robert Morgan says, "*Bledsoe* reads like a poem by Cormac McCarthy," he pays highest praise to both the stylistic intensity and the conceptual architecture of the book. To have all these poems together in one volume, and to be able to follow the arc from the beginning to the present, is a gift to readers of poetry, and Mercer University Press should be gratefully acknowledged for recognizing the importance of this work.

Can readers know poets through their work? Who is William Wright? I really should be able to answer, as he has been my closest working companion for more than a dozen years. We wrote a book of poems together and have co-edited three volumes of *The Southern Poetry Anthology* series. We have given readings, taught workshops, and taken road trips together, and we have been part of the same writing group with Dan Morris and James Clinton Howell for a decade. The person *Will* is just as encyclopedic in his knowledge and interests as the speaker of these poems, but he is also funnier. A typical phone conversation with Will might last an hour or two and range from making a list of favorite American poems since 1970 to how to repair a mechanical wristwatch, from the medical issues of our parents to fractals, astrophysics, and quantum mechanics. Will is a video game aficionado, and he built his own computer once from scratch; he is a lover of Baroque music and surrealist visual art and a student of cosmology and consciousness. He loves languages and has translated the German poet Georg Trakl, among others, into English. The last book he recommended to me wasn't some little-known poetry volume but *Parable of the Sower* by Octavia Butler (I loved it, just as he predicted). When I try to connect the threads of all Will has read and watched and listened to, I feel like John Livingston Lowes furiously tracing the sources of Coleridge's imagination in *The Road to Xanadu*. I know it is an impossible journey, yet what an adventure!

Wright is a younger poet today than either Robert Frost or Wallace Stevens when they published their first volumes. Despite all that these poems have accomplished, a reader anticipates what might lie ahead. In a comment for his 2013 chapbook, *Xylem & Heartwood*, I wrote, "William Wright is the young American poet most likely to discover a new way to frame the deep paradoxes of life and language shown before by Coleridge, by Rilke, and by James Wright." As I read his new poems, I feel more certain of this claim than ever. Consider these lines from the poem "Anodyne":

> so that nights
> when I can't sleep,
> I can ride out
>
> those creatures'
> compound melodies,
> their one and only hymn.

Such lines offer proof of the deepening well of his inspiration. William Wright invokes the Muses. They sing.

15

In Exchange: Interviews

With William Wright for *Town Creek Poetry*
(Spring 2007)

WRIGHT: Can you speak about your literary forbears? Who has influenced your work, and what writers continue to haunt you?

GRAVES: There are poets whose work steadily holds my attention, and more than that, particular books of poems. I've got a shelf of contemporary poetry books that continue to reveal themselves to me, including Charles Wright's *The Southern Cross*, Robert Morgan's *At the Edge of Orchard Country*, Jack Gilbert's *The Great Fires*, Stanley Plumly's *The Boy on the Step*, Linda Gregg's *Chosen by the Lion*, and Robert Hass's *Human Wishes*—I hate even to end the list. Despite some stylistic differences, you might notice that all these poets work with an engagement with landscape, a quest for meaning, and an examination of personal relationships, and that these concerns form the foundation for most of their work. I am aware that I work from a distinct train of influence—you might call it the line of Romanticism. My sensibilities are more Wordsworth than Byron, more Whitman than Dickinson, more Frost than Stevens, more Machado than

Vallejo, which is not to say, for instance, that I think Dickinson is less of a poet than Whitman; trying to prove that is a fool's errand.

Well, I did grow up in Appalachia, and I do have a kind of identification with the experiences that others writers from this region have written about. More so than with Jack Gilbert or Louise Glück? In some ways, yes; in other ways, such as Gilbert's search for an adequate emotional vocabulary, as in "The Hidden Dialect of the Heart," or Glück's sense of voice in the inanimate in her *Wild Iris* poems, not really. A really important component of Appalachian writing is how site-specific the literature is, and I respond to that in Thomas Hardy or James Joyce, just as I do in James Still. Here again I think the notion of setting is important in what has influenced me.

Insights and recognitions reveal themselves in various ways, and I tend to connect more with the indirect and the woven than with the sarcastic or the explosive. I'm not a storyteller in my work, necessarily, but there is a definite narrative thread—my poems are mostly about things that happen to people.

WRIGHT: In Tony Hoagland's recent book of essays, *Real Sofistikashun*, he comments on the "skittery poem of our moment," the poem of meaningless meanings, of purposeful obfuscation (one might call Ashbery the "father" of such work). Your poems, and much of the poetry that is written in your region, tend to be entrenched in an unspoken battle with this aesthetic. Can you comment on why this might be the case?

GRAVES: It is wonderfully appropriate that you would mention John Ashbery as the opposite of what my poems are going for, as I am just this week revising a paper on Ashbery to send to my old professor Roger Gilbert. It's called "The Single Seam in *The Double Dream of Spring*: Ashbery's Natural Sublime," and in it I argue that the use of landscape has been much overlooked in the commentary on Ashbery's work, but that he dislocates the speaker's response to the landscape in a manner very distinct from Charles Wright or W. S. Merwin or other contemporaries associated with natural imagery. Basically, that Ashbery is a landscape artist, just a nonrepresentational, non-mimetic one.

I tend to have a big-tent, utilitarian view of poetry, in that there ought to be room for as many approaches as poets are inclined toward. Obviously, I don't value them all equally, and though I might prefer the emotional openness and authenticity of Jane Hirschfield, I can still appreciate the sardonic wit of Charles Simic or the crystalline economy of Michael Palmer. I suppose that if I identified myself with a more avant-garde approach, I would need to be more exclusionary in my poetics, but a commitment to the poem of Meaningless Meanings seems as limiting to me as committing to writing nothing but straight English sonnets from here on out.

I am familiar with Tony Hoagland's essay on the "skittery poem of our moment" and actually reference it in my essay on Robert Morgan and Ron Rash in *Southern Quarterly*. He seems exactly right to me about the trend in American poetry toward a kind of surface mobility and mere witticism. However, poems are not short stories, and they suffer when they give away too much of their mystery, which is a problem with lots of narrative poetry. The best narrative poets, like Dave Smith and B. H. Fairchild, are still writing with lyric concision and an openness that permits surprise and mystery into their work, and their poems feel neither boxed in nor mundane like the work of some narrative poets.

WRIGHT: You have just published a prominent essay in *Southern Quarterly* about the formal elements in the work of Ron Rash and Robert Morgan. As a poet who vacillates between writing poems and academic essays, how do you view the role of the poet in the academy and vice versa? Does academic writing facilitate your creative work or serve as an obstacle?

GRAVES: I think poets have always been the most sensitive critics of poetry and have provided the best commentary on the art, at least as far back as Horace. Contemporary theory and criticism hardly engages poetry at all, and when critics do write about poetry, it is often as part of a social construct or a political/language paradigm. Poets are free to write about the aesthetics of poetry, and that prospect interests me greatly as both a reader and an analyst of the art form. I care a great deal about politics, and about social structures and identities, but I don't think art should be subjugated to the study of them. The kind of criticism I admire takes poetry for its own value and makes a careful study of its history, its ways and means, and its objectives.

The academy does offer a great gift to a writer, which is time. Poetry is not a spontaneous art for me, and teaching allows for some flexibility in the time I can give to a poem's development. There are also not that many jobs for a person with a poet's traditional skill set—reading comprehension, written and verbal expression. I suppose I could have become a lawyer, which seems not all that different from being a teacher to me, except of course for the salary. Nearly as important as time for a writer, though, is the nearness to literature's history that the university provides. The University of Tennessee has a world-class research library and a pretty fair collection of contemporary poetry and periodicals. I admit also that I enjoy being around so many people for part of the week—for one who pursues solitary work, the energy of young people in a crowd can be a source of renewal.

WRIGHT: Where do you see your poetry going? That is, what aesthetic changes are currently taking place in your work?

GRAVES: The past few months have felt like a period of growth in my work, and I can't really attribute it to any particular event or revelation. I am working now on a longer piece, a narrative poem set in the 1970s, in a voice that could be my older brother's, but it isn't necessarily about any particular thing that happened to him—he just provides a model. This is interesting for me, as most of my poems have come out of my own range of experiences and are written in a generally consistent voice. I have been able to work with some truly great teachers in my time as a student of poetry, including Robert Morgan and A. R. Ammons at Cornell, who represent a couple of the most persuasive directions in contemporary poetry to me. Here at UT, I've been able to work again with Arthur Smith and Marilyn Kallet, who guided my undergraduate work as well, and who know my writing from the very beginning. I had one life-direction-changing term with the great Jack Gilbert when he was visiting writer at UT, which reconnected me with writing poetry at a time when I was leaning more heavily toward scholarship. Writing poetry always comes to me with a certain amount of the anxiety of the unknown, and lately that has been more thrilling than usual—I'll take that as a sign of the natural sources of the work. Either that, or else I have taken William Stafford's suggestion about lowering one's standards in order to write every day a step too far.

With Denton Loving for *Chapter 16*
(April 2012)

LOVING: Congratulations on your first collection of poetry called *Tennessee Landscape with Blighted Pine*. How long have you been writing and revising the poems that make up this collection?

GRAVES: Thanks, Denton. I've been working on this first book of poems for several years. Some of these poems go back to 1999 or 2000, though most that made it into the book are more recent than that. I decided seven or eight years ago that I wasn't going to rush my first book into print, and I'm happy now that I was patient enough to wait for the right poems to come together.

LOVING: When did you start writing, and what led you to pursue writing poetry?

GRAVES: I started writing in high school, or maybe even middle school, but back then I thought I was writing songs. It turns out I wasn't a natural musician and that what I really liked were the lyrics to my favorite songs, how they could evoke an image or a feeling or tell a story. I guess that I was in college before I realized that what I really loved was poetry and started seriously trying to write it.

LOVING: Who are some of your favorite poets, and how do you think they've influenced your own poetry?

GRAVES: I have some favorite "classic" poets, especially Walt Whitman, Emily Dickinson, and Robert Frost in America, and William Wordsworth, John Keats, and Rainer Maria Rilke from abroad. I read lots of contemporary poetry, though, and many of my favorites are from the South, including Robert Morgan, Charles Wright, and David Bottoms. I have found that because my subject matter is often similar to those poets, reading poems from other cultures helps me to keep a large canvas open for my own work. Lately I have been reading some French poets in translation, especially enjoying Arthur Rimbaud and Jean Follain, and also the Polish poet Adam Zagajewski.

LOVING: One of the most noticeable themes throughout the collection is how you draw on your family—individuals and your relationship to those individuals, as well as the family as a whole and your family's over two-hundred-year history in East Tennessee. How do you manage to write about your family without being overly sentimental?

GRAVES: I hope I mostly avoid sentimentality, but my work tends pretty close to the line. I had the chance as a graduate student to study with Jack Gilbert, one of the truly great American poets, who was a visiting writer at UT. He gave me some advice about this that I've never forgotten: he said that sentimentality was the risk most worth taking in poetry. He meant that what you feel strongest about is what your poems should be about, and that to avoid that is to leave the real feelings out of the work.

LOVING: Your poems evidence a clear sense of place, much of which happens to be physically located in Appalachia. Do you think of yourself as an Appalachian poet or a poet from any particular tradition?

GRAVES: I feel happy to be associated with Appalachia and proud of that as my cultural heritage. Most writers want to stay away from labels that might simplify their work, and I hope that people don't make too many assumptions about my poems because of where I'm from. The tradition of lyric poetry I relate to includes writers from all over the world, Appalachia included.

LOVING: I stress the sense of place in your work because it's so strong. How conscious are you about sense of place or any other elements when you're creating?

GRAVES: Place is part of the sensual world that inspires my writing. I've said before that if I were from Memphis, Tennessee, instead of Sharps Chapel, Tennessee, my poems would still be just as much about place, and environment, as they are now, because that is innate to my sensibility. The imagery would probably be different, but the emphasis would be the same—I'm sure of it.

LOVING: You received the Master of Fine Arts from Cornell University. And you've taught at The University of New Orleans. How did it affect your writing about the region to leave it for some time? And how does it affect your work now that you've returned to the region?

GRAVES: I think living outside the region for five years gave me a wonderful opportunity to see my homeplace in perspective, to contrast it with the landscape and lifestyles in a couple of really distinctive places. It was also important for me to miss East Tennessee for a while, to think about it from a distance and consider what I loved about it. In some ways, I felt very comfortable in a place like Ithaca, New York, where there is a great university with a real culture of books and learning, where curiosity is prized and not considered with suspicion, where the politics feel more humane than here at home.

LOVING: You teach creative writing at East Tennessee State University, and you also teach poetry workshops, including at the prestigious Appalachian Writers Workshop. What do you enjoy about helping other poets hone their craft, especially undergraduate students at ETSU?

GRAVES: I love teaching, in every setting and with every group of students I've experienced. I know I've been given a real gift to get to work at something I love and that feels so natural. Teaching and writing are a perfect complement to me, because I feel both social and solitary in pretty much equal measure. I have arrived at ETSU at a really special moment, when we have an incredible group of writing students and where we have an opportunity to build on an already strong community. I've had such great teachers in my time, including Kenneth Venable in high school and David Worley in my first year of college at LMU, that I truly believe that great teachers can change lives. So for me, teaching has been a way to try and give something back for all the gifts my teachers have given me.

LOVING: *Tennessee Landscape with Blighted Pine* was the 2011 recipient of the prestigious Weatherford Award, and it's also been very well received by many major poets. How does that sort of validation drive or influence your work?

GRAVES: The Weatherford Award was a wonderful surprise, and a real upset I would say, given that some of my favorite poets had new books nominated! The validation has felt really good, I admit, though I would quickly point out that many truly great poets (Emily Dickinson, for example) never received any outside validation at all, so the real gratification for a poet has to come from within, from knowing you've made the best work you can make out of what you've been given to work with.

LOVING: Besides your own writing, you've done considerable work as an editor (a previous anthology from the Knoxville Writers Guild, as well as recent and forthcoming volumes of *The Southern Poetry Anthology*). What's it like for you to work as an editor? Is it easy or difficult for you to switch gears from poet to editor and back again?

GRAVES: Editing feels like a pretty natural extension of my writing and teaching, and a way to pursue the first love that brought me to literature so many years ago, and that is reading. Editing is time-intensive work, so it really has to be a labor of love. New reading has always generated new writing for me, so in that way, editorial work has nourished my own writing.

LOVING: Do you write in any genres besides poetry? If so, what? If not, do you have any interest in doing so?

GRAVES: I have written quite a few essays through the years, and like the editing work, that has given me lots to think about for my own creative writing, which I always consider as my primary work. I like having several projects in mind at once, so that if I get stalled on one thing, I can move on to another. I don't mean that I am multitasking—when I'm writing a poem, it has my full attention—only that I'm comfortable with shifting gears. I probably learned this from my mom in the kitchen, who has always been a great cook, or from my dad on the farm, who has always been able to fix anything that needed it.

LOVING: What are you writing now, and what will we see from you next?

GRAVES: I am almost always working on poems, so I hope eventually I will have a second book of poetry. I like to sit with poems and get to know them before trying to publish them, so I don't really have a timetable for it. The next thing should be a book of essays on Robert Morgan's writing that I am currently co-editing with an excellent scholar at Mississippi State named Robert West. The book is tentatively called *Time's Music: Essays on the Poetry and Prose of Robert Morgan*, and it will be published by McFarland Publishers out of North Carolina. This will be the first book on Morgan's work, and it has some great essays by renowned scholars and also some great pictures of Morgan and his family.

LOVING: What advice do you give to young or emerging poets?

GRAVES: Poetry requires a long apprenticeship. I always encourage young poets to be patient and persistent, to persevere, even if the poems haven't yet reached their potential. Most importantly, read as much as you can—find a favorite poet or two, and read everything they ever wrote, but also read broadly, so that you see how vast the possibilities are for this art form. Try to understand even the poems you don't like, because they might teach you something. It also helps to find a friend, someone who will read your poems honestly and encouragingly—poems get written in solitude, but they thrive in community.

With Nathanial Perry for
Hampden-Sydney Poetry Review (2013)

PERRY: In his well-known 1935 introduction to E. A. Robinson's mostly forgotten book-length poem, *King Jasper*, Robert Frost reminds the reader why we haven't forgotten the others of Robinson's poems. In doing so he lays out a basic premise—that art should not, or maybe cannot, merely engage a grievance but should instead express a grief. For him, this distinction between "grief" and "grievance" becomes a sword with which he at once slices apart a lot of the contemporary poetry he sees around him and lifts up (by its point, one presumes) Robinson's understated (and underrated) verse. What would you say to this distinction (and, I suppose, value judgment) between "grief" and "grievance" in poetry?

GRAVES: I think of "grief" as the essential element in elegy, and most of our great lyric poems fall into one or the other (and sometimes it's hard to tell which) of the classic modes of the ode or the elegy. If sorrow is the principal aspect of grief, and complaint is the main portion of grievance, then it is easy for me to agree with Frost's value judgment. Grievance suggests a topical problem, and a subject that is unlikely to age well, sometimes dated before even a decade passes. I think Frost wanted to indicate a timeless quality in Robinson's work by making the distinction that his work evoked authentic grief in the reader, that his poetry was and would remain "the real thing," as Henry James called it.

Except for the occasional reaction toward political crisis or malfeasance, like *Poets against the War* in the previous administration, I don't see much contemporary poetry of grievance. In fact, I think we may be seeing an overcorrection against the Confessional mode, to the extent that the lyric "I" has come under suspicion and often derision. This risks losing one of the key elements to ode and the elegy, which is that the lyric "I" is a crucial way to invest value and significance, to give the speaker, and consequently the reader, something at stake in the poem. No one feels generic grief, or anonymous grief, and as the local detail can generate universality, so can personal grief invoke meaningful sorrow.

PERRY: There is a particular moment in the essay when Frost declares that "grievances" are impatient and that "grief" is, in turn, patient. Or that to engage grief properly in poetry, one must be or exhibit patience. This turn in Frost's thinking has been making me think about a broader notion of patience in poetry. What might your thoughts be? What good is patience as a writer? Can you imagine a poetics of impatience that succeeds? How might this play out in your own work?

GRAVES: I am always preaching patience to my students, and letting not only their poems but also the voices and visions for their poems develop over time. This was my own practice for years, and I believe it was what I needed to learn to write poems. Some of the poems in my first book evolved for a decade or more before being published. If I could replace "impatience" with "spontaneity," then I could certainly subscribe to the value of that. In fact, about three times a year, a small group of poet friends and I write a poem a day for a month, and I can honestly say that it's transformed my approach to writing poems. Not surprisingly, I don't get a good poem every day through that process, but in my experience, good poems arrive to me in batches. I feel like an athlete who gets in "the zone." I can recognize the material for poems better, and bring a more perceptive kind of energy to the material, when I am obliged to go for it every day. Lots of poets I admire seem to have embraced an element of spontaneity in their work—Jack Spicer and Robert Creeley come to mind, and more recently Larry Levis, Robert Hass, and Jane Hirshfield.

PERRY: At the end of the piece, Frost gives us his final criterion—that while a poem must sing of grief, must give the reader, as he puts it "immedicable woes," it must, while doing so, play. "The play's the thing. Play's the thing," he writes famously—in the face of insoluble danger, dilemma, mystery, pain, etc., the poet must play. Is this, for you, an apt description of the artist's charge? Is poetry, in a way, a kind of dancing on the deck of a foundering ship? Agreeing or disagreeing with Frost, how does play or playfulness factor into your own work and/or your conception of poetry?

GRAVES: This question makes me think of a later poem from Jack Gilbert called "Metier," which I will quote in its entirety: "The Greek fishermen do not / play on the beach and I don't / write funny poems." Gilbert is one of my poetry gurus, and I probably take his word on this too much to heart, or maybe he became a central poet to me because he feels this way. I have had unreasonable good fortune in poetry teachers, and I had the chance to study under Gilbert for a semester when I was a new grad student at Tennessee in 2004. I sat with him at a fiction reading by Barry Hannah, which had a full auditorium roaring with laughter, yet at the end when I asked Gilbert if he enjoyed the reading, he flatly said, "No. I don't do this for entertainment."

I suppose I'm disagreeing with Frost (and Auden) here, which I doubt I would do very often on matters of poetry. For me, a little play in poems goes a long way. "Home Burial" is a much greater poem, to me, than "Mending Wall." In fact, I'd say "Home Burial" is one of the half-dozen greatest American poems. As Wallace Stevens proves, there is lots of room in great poetry for play, but again, I'll take "Sunday Morning" or "The Snow Man" over "The Emperor of Ice Cream." I wouldn't give play so central a role as Frost claims for it.

I sometimes wish I wrote more funny poems, especially when I read to an audience. I love to laugh, and maybe there are a few wry moments in my work, but it wouldn't take me long to count them. *Annie Hall* is my favorite movie. I could watch Christopher Walken on *Saturday Night Live* for hours. And yet the kind of hyper-ironic, witty, urbane poetry that has been so popular in America, among younger poets especially, doesn't appeal to me at all. I see it as a way of evading the real issues of people's lives, and ultimately of not taking people seriously. Poetry, for me, is the opposite of escapism.

PERRY: Frost wasn't really propping up Robinson's reputation with this piece (he was still quite famous), but to contemporary eyes it reads like it. What undeservedly unappreciated poet would you want to write a similar introduction for? What would you say? What, in his or her poetics, speaks, as Robinson's did for Frost, to the larger aims of poetry and art as you see them?

GRAVES: I'm wary of filing a grievance here rather than taking up a grief. Poets from my part of the country—we could call it the Mountain South, or Southern Appalachia—have met with some difficulty in finding an audience outside the region. I teach an American Poetry class with the *Oxford Book of American Poetry*, and the only poet included who is from or who has long-standing ties to the region is the undeniable Charles Wright. No Robert Morgan, no Fred Chappell, no Kathryn Stripling Byer. I wish the poems of Louise McNeill, Jonathan Williams, and Jeff Daniel Marion were all better known outside Appalachia.

If I had the power of Frost to introduce only one poet to a broader audience, I would choose George Scarbrough, whose disappearance from the national poetry conversation gives me real grief. Scarbrough was born in 1915 and published his first book with Dutton in 1949, and many of his poems appeared in *Poetry* and other prestigious journals. He died only recently, living virtually his entire life in East Tennessee. His early poems are nearly impossible to find, and his later poems are only available because of the heroic efforts of East Tennessee's Iris Press.

Scarbrough wrote about sorrowful situations, like growing up in abject rural poverty, and with a difficult unsympathetic father, who became a sort of ambivalent muse to Scarbrough. In my estimation, any reader of Richard Wilbur, Theodore Roethke, or Elizabeth Bishop would find lots to admire in George Scarbrough's poetry. Scarbrough's writing is often as graceful as Wilbur's or Bishop's, but he doesn't fear the darker reaches of the psyche, and he shares Roethke's courage to peer into the depths. He wrote about nature and animals with startling empathy and insight, and about his deprived childhood in language both elegant and sonorous. Scarbrough is a treasure worth searching for and, in keeping with the earlier questions, a true poetic descendant of Frost and Robinson.

With Alexandra Taylor for *Roanoke Review* (2017)

TAYLOR: The language you use in your poetry is beautiful. I particularly enjoyed the moments in "Trace": "cardiac pulsing of a transmission" and "as the vanishing of a name / forgotten whispers not even a soft goodbye." What inspired you to write this poem?

GRAVES: Thanks, Alex, for noticing those particular lines. "Trace" was written as part of a sequence I was working on with a friend, and it picks up a fairly persistent theme for me, that so much of the knowledge we acquire over time slips away. I spent hours and hours as a kid (and as an adult) learning about specific things—in the poem, it's the names of car parts and how they work together—and then interests change, or focus moves to something else, and I lose that information. One of the great things about writing is that it gives us an occasion to make a record of what we don't want to let go, a means for keeping a kind of hold on memories and experiences.

TAYLOR: "Not at War" has a nostalgic nature, and it addresses the college experience. How has your education impacted your writing career?

GRAVES: College was a revelation to me. I loved being in a place where so many people wanted to talk about books, and that there were classes that facilitated those conversations. It was the group-oriented time of my life. "Not at War" is nostalgic for youth, certainly, and also a particular time in public life. I was an undergraduate in the 1990s, before 9/11, the Iraq War, and the Wall Street bailouts and financial collapse. It was even before social media as we know it now! I was a first-generation college student from a working-class background, so I faced some challenges in finding my way through university life, but it was worth the struggle because it gave me a community I needed. Many students don't feel safe on college campuses, and that's a source of real sadness for me, because I know that if the environment is right, wonderful things can happen for people.

TAYLOR: We last saw you when you published two poems, "Taylor's Grove," and "West of Raleigh," in Issue 27 of the *Roanoke Review*. How have you changed as a writer since then?

GRAVES: Well, the time has flown! I think I have gotten more patient as a writer, and as I've read more, and thought more about poetry, I hope the canvas I work with has gotten a little larger. Some of my poems have taken a long time to develop, and I feel better about the work when I don't rush it into being, or out into the world. I suspect, though, that I still have a lot of the same inclinations I had back in Issue 27—I prefer a lyrical style, and I care about landscape and how people interact with one another.

TAYLOR: What writers have influenced you throughout your career? How have they impacted your craft practices?

GRAVES: James Wright was a very important early influence for me, for reasons that were both aesthetic and cultural. His poems were lyrical yet retained a kind of raw energy and exploratory persistence that I admired. I could also tell from his work, and the bit of biographical information I could find, that his background had been something like my own, and that might have connected me to his work in a more personal way. Philip Levine and Larry Levis have been similar influences for me. I am definitely interested in the formal elements of poetry, the components that make up the practice of poetry. Some of the scholarship I have done focuses on the craft of making poems, such as the use of syllabics as a way of measuring the poetic line, or the relation between song lyrics and poems. More recently, I have found Adam Zagajewski's and Gjertrud Schnackenberg's work to be seemingly endless of interest and inspiration. Stylistically, they feel pretty different, with Zagajewski's interest in phenomenology and Schnackenberg's more metaphysical turn, but both write poems of deep feeling, clarity, and formal beauty.

TAYLOR: As a teacher of writing, what is the most important lesson you try to impart to your students?

GRAVES: I hope that I have encouraged my students to trust their own perceptions and their own voices, and to always be open to new perspectives on their subject matter. Since I came to ETSU in 2009, I've been lucky to work with an almost unbelievable string of talented student writers, and I have tried to meet their poems where they are and to assist them toward being the kind of poems they want to become. So many wonderful teachers have influenced my work, on poems and in the classroom, that a few, like Connie Jordan Green, Marilyn Kallet, Kenneth McClane, Robert Morgan, and Arthur Smith, should be mentioned by name. They are also all wonderful poets, who each helped me find a way into my own material.

TAYLOR: Your family has a long legacy in Tennessee. How does your personal and family history factor into your writing?

GRAVES: My family roots in rural East Tennessee have provided a good deal of subject matter for my poems, both in terms of the visual imagery of old houses and woodlands and farm life and in the narratives of the lives of people who often go unrecorded. My graduate school professor, Robert Morgan, uses a phrase that has made a deep impression on me: he says that in reading and writing about the past, we create "a community across time." I really love that idea, that we can share a bond with those who came before us (and those who come after, too, I suppose), and that we can read their stories and also tell our versions of the stories they may not have been able to tell for themselves.

TAYLOR: Why do you write?

GRAVES: I like the way words sound together—that must have been the initial reason, and it probably still makes the truest answer for me. Music was my gateway into poetry, and I love those same pleasurable aspects of language. I also like to try to record impressions of what I see and experience, and to make connections between those things that help me to understand what they might mean. Poems have a special way of communicating, through figures of speech and a dazzling range of sound effects, and each poet is free to find his or her own voice within the poems. I find that if I want to explore a thought or a feeling, and if I can keep open to perceptions and associations, unexpected things can happen. Images appear that I might not have expected, patterns emerge in phrases or structural elements, or I might feel something about the subject that I didn't know I felt. I find the possibility of the unwritten poem irresistible.

With Linda Parsons for *Chapter 16* (2021)[1]

An Unbroken Thread: Poet Jesse Graves discusses his fourth collection, *Merciful Days*

By Linda Parsons

These days especially, we crave mercy, that plenitude both given and received in times of loss and uncertainty. Such benevolence and kindness infuse East Tennessee poet Jesse Graves's fourth collection, *Merciful Days*, titled with an expression his mother used often. Despite his many losses—father, brother, a favorite uncle—Graves is rarely alone in his native valleys and ridges of Sharps Chapel in Union County, ancestral land rich with the spirits and stories of great-greats and beyond, each "a broad old footprint."

In haunting lyric poems and traditional narratives, Graves shows us these "ghost-lives" that shaped the boy learning the rough language of cows and that imprint the returning adult who walks the fence line now without his father. He slows our busyness and distraction, draws us into time's shimmer in this particular place, his childhood's almost mythical forest and cove where "the world held us like a cup," where history and even prehistory move like a "nameless river."

It is fitting that this book was released in October, when the veil is traditionally believed thinnest between the present and the otherworld, for Graves seems as familiar with the other side as with the sage grass at his feet. And fitting to clasp the locket of these elegies close, like a reunion photograph with his beloved dead appearing like "eternals," yet fleeting and taking those merciful days with them. In fact, the striking cover with its murmuration of swallows vibrates in motion, those shades of remembrance weaving above us, "a sound like wind / coming to life." Yes, now more than ever, bring us mercy. Bring us the enduring, healing power of

---

[1] Published as "An Unbroken Thread: Poet Jesse Graves discusses his fourth collection, *Merciful Days*," interview by Linda Parsons, *Chapter 16*, January 11, 2021.

home to reconcile the lost with the found in our lives.

Note: I've known Jesse Graves for many years, since he was an undergraduate at The University of Tennessee, Knoxville. I've admired his poetry and critical work as it deepened over time and am proud of his work now as poet-in-residence and professor of literature and creative writing at East Tennessee State University. He answered questions for *Chapter 16* via email.

CHAPTER 16: You navigate many losses in *Merciful Days* while keeping a careful balance between emotion and restraint. Are you conscious of maintaining that balance and avoiding sentimentality in your work, especially in memory poems?

GRAVES: Thank you for recognizing the balance that I am continually hoping to maintain. I realize the danger of sentimentality with my subject matter, and even with my way of seeing and processing the world. A lot of people and places I care about are gone and are not coming back. I always remember something the great Jack Gilbert said in response to a poem of mine in workshop: "Sentimentality is the risk most worth taking in poetry." He said that poets should be willing to go where their real feelings take them, because that is where the most important discoveries can be made in poetry. I have realized through the years that most of the poems I really love, and truly care about, from passages of *The Odyssey* to Joy Harjo's "Remember," take that risk.

CHAPTER 16: Writing in times of loss can move our emotions outside of ourselves as we shape a poem or story—and often helps us travel through grief to a place of acceptance. Did writing these poems help in your grieving process?

GRAVES: Writing and revising these poems did help me manage my grief over the loss of close family members, though it sometimes takes a while for me to see how the poems will come together. One of the poems from early in the book, "Nameless River," seems now like a fairly straightforward memory poem about trying to recover a name from my dad's past, but it was the hardest poem in the whole book for me to figure out.

Trying to articulate all that was lost to me when my dad passed felt too daunting to even ponder, but I desperately needed to recall that name, the man who gave my dad his first independent opportunity. I realized that for every puzzle I solved, countless others would remain in fragments, but I felt a deep connection to my dad when I unearthed the name of Clyde Ivey, who died many years before I was born but was important to me nevertheless.

I have thought of *Merciful Days* as the book of my mother's voice, and the title phrase comes from an expression of her grief, which is an essential part of what we have shared and a weight we have tried to carry together.

CHAPTER 16: In setting much of your poetry in your native Tennessee community of Sharps Chapel, you've created a microcosm that contains the universe—much as fellow Tennessean Charles Wright does from the view of his land in Montana. Could you share your thoughts on the relationship between the particular and the universal? How do you navigate that relationship in your writing?

GRAVES: Thank you for that encouraging comment. Charles Wright has been one of my favorite poets for most of my writing life, and I have learned so much about how poems can be put together from reading his work. I am sure that I was subconsciously imitating Wright for a decade or more, only to finally realize that his genius was not a transferable skill! I have been reading Catharine Savage Brosman's New Mexico and New Orleans poems recently, which were a gift from my Louisiana poet friend John Freeman. I find a beautiful sense of place in many of her individual poems, but I also feel a larger canvas that somehow unites them, that I think must simply be her specific voice and sensibility.

I've wondered about this issue through the years and always considered that Seamus Heaney's poems were the perfect model of getting to a universal understanding through the particular individual experience. I relate to his poems so directly, though I've never been to Ireland, much less to Mossbawn, and yet it feels as real to me as my own Sharps Chapel.

CHAPTER 16: Following that line of thought, how is your work fully of the southern Appalachian region yet transcending the region?

GRAVES: I believe I would probably limit the range where my work represents with any authority down to the locations in East Tennessee I have written about, my homeplace in Union County, a few parts of Knoxville,

Johnson City, and the Roan Mountain area. I never really came across the idea of Appalachian literature until I was in college, reading Lee Smith's fiction in Dr. George Hutchinson's Intro to American Studies course at UT.

I also wrote my first real personal essay in that class, about my ancestors in Sharps Chapel, of course. It was called "History of a Small World." I don't think my family really identified as natives of Appalachia when I was growing up, but just as general country people. I think there is some continuity in those rural experiences—I felt them in college when I read *The Woodlanders* by Thomas Hardy and *O Pioneers* by Willa Cather, and more recently in the fiction and essays of the English pastoralist Richard Jefferies. I hope that readers from anywhere and everywhere would find something to relate to in the lives I have written about and in the places I know most personally.

CHAPTER 16: There are ghost stories and haints galore in *Merciful Days*. How do hauntings work in your writing, especially as grounded in Appalachian traditions?

GRAVES: Well, I was raised in a traditional Appalachian "dark holler," where we could not see or hear our nearest neighbors and the road that passed was named for an early nineteenth-century woman believed to have been a witch. I love the folklore of the community, but I also had a spooky enough childhood to not be willing to say for sure that none of it is true. I cannot explain all that I have seen.

Ghost stories, though, are not only about the past for me. I have been fascinated for years by this concept of "hauntology," which originates with Jacques Derrida's *Specters of Marx*, and the idea of "lost futures" as described Mark Fisher, who talked about a nostalgia for all the possible futures that have been closed off to us by circumstance. I see it all around when I visit Sharps Chapel. I calculated this recently: nearly half of the boys from my tiny elementary school who were in my grade, and one grade above and below me, have spent time in prison or have died. It feels eerie to think about a vanished generation and the haunted state of being they have left behind.

CHAPTER 16: Numerous poems also spring from waking dreams and dreams of sleep, both yours and your mother's. Writing from dreams can be tricky, whether to shape them as surreal or realistic. How do dreams take you further into the heart of your poems' mysteries?

GRAVES: It's funny you should mention this idea—the manuscript of poems I was writing alongside the *Merciful Days* poems is tentatively called *Across the River of Waking Dreams*. I don't believe I have mentioned that to anyone, so I don't think you could have known. Those kinds of symmetries further convince me that a poet's world is mostly a dream world. The mind I am in when I write my poems feels somewhere in between the way I feel when I am asleep and dreaming and when I am awake and working on other things like grading papers or buying groceries. In my own experience, poems are like dreams, kind of elusive, and they need a lot of room to run around before I can settle them down into words. A poem can escape just as quickly as a dream fleets away after waking up.

CHAPTER 16: In the poem "Wind Work," you indirectly mention the coming of Norris Dam/Norris Lake, which submerged your family's land. How has this loss reverberated through your family generationally, and what metaphors does it bring to your writing?

GRAVES: The changes brought by the TVA's Norris projects have been a persistent theme in my writing—the title of my second book of poems, *Basin Ghosts*, comes from a line in a poem about the TVA removals. Those changes are fundamental and ongoing, too, with most of the new development in Sharps Chapel happening in gated communities on the banks of Norris Lake. It amounts to a kind of rural gentrification that I haven't seen written about very much.

I think the effects on my family gave me a sense of the impermanence of living in place. The land itself changes, and our relationship to it can change drastically and suddenly even if we do not want it to happen. It also helped me to think about how Sharps Chapel was contested land and about the Native people who lived here before my ancestors arrived. When I was a child, it was thrilling to dig around in the creek beds and find arrowheads, but it gave me a sense, even then, of how much things could change over time.

CHAPTER 16: You have studied with poets Jack Gilbert, Robert Morgan, and Arthur Smith and interviewed Charles Wright and David Madden.

How would you say your work is in conversation with other works of literature, both within and outside the Appalachian region?

GRAVES: I sometimes cannot believe the good fortune I have had with teachers in my life and with my opportunities to learn directly from amazing writers. Connie Jordan Green was my first poetry instructor at UT, followed by the true dream team of Marilyn Kallet and Arthur Smith, whose styles and approaches were perfectly complementary for a young poet to learn from. I studied with Robert Morgan and Kenneth McClane at Cornell, and to me, Morgan is the quintessential writer of Appalachian experience. I got to know A. R. Ammons, too, who was semi-retired but came to campus every morning to visit with whoever wandered by the Temple of Zeus coffeeshop in Goldwin Smith Hall. Ammons gave me one of the best pieces of advice I ever got for my poetry, and one of the simplest: He said, "You need more hard sounds in these poems." At that time, I was a young poet stoked about Hart Crane and John Keats, in love with pure lyricism, and those early poems of mine needed an edge to them.

Every writer has their own lineage of the books they have read, the teachers they have learned from, the readings and conversations and bookstores that have shaped them. I suppose I am writing back to say thank you to Walt Whitman and Emily Dickinson just as much to Robert Morgan, who helped me choose the poems for *Merciful Days*. Literature feels like an unbroken thread, connecting people through time and across continents, and that has helped me understand the continuities and the particularities of my life. I hope my own writing is an expression of gratitude to those who made the effort to leave a record of what they experienced in their times and places.